Anthony
with JOE BROWNE
Browne

PLAYING THE SHAPE GAME

To our family

Plc and endpaper illustration: *Willy's Pictures,* Walker Books, 2000

Title Page: *The Shape Game,* Doubleday, 2003

Introduction illustration: *The Shape Game,* Doubleday, 2003

PLAYING THE SHAPE GAME
A DOUBLEDAY BOOK 978 0 385 61050 6
Published in Great Britain by Doubleday,
an imprint of Random House Children's Books
A Random House Group Company

This edition published 2011

1 3 5 7 9 10 8 6 4 2

Text copyright © Anthony Browne and Joe Browne, 2011
Illustrations copyright © Anthony Browne except where noted

The Acknowledgements on page 240 constitute an extension of this copyright notice

The right of Anthony Browne and Joe Browne to be identified as the authors and illustrator of this
book has been asserted in accordance with the Copyright, Designs and Patents Act 1988.

RANDOM HOUSE CHILDREN'S BOOKS
61–63 Uxbridge Road, London W5 5SA

www.kidsatrandomhouse.co.uk
www.rbooks.co.uk

Addresses for companies within The Random House Group Limited can be found at:
www.randomhouse.co.uk/offices.htm

THE RANDOM HOUSE GROUP Limited Reg. No. 954009

A CIP catalogue record for this book is available from the British Library.

Printed and bound in China

Anthony Browne

with JOE BROWNE

Browne

Playing the Shape Game

DOUBLEDAY

Contents

Introduction

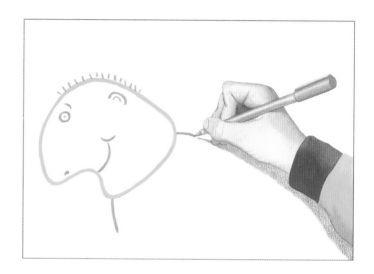

The idea for this book was suggested some years ago by Julia MacRae, my editor for the first twenty years of my career. I started work on it many times but couldn't get beyond the word 'I'. It seemed so pretentious writing, 'I did this . . .' or, 'I did that . . .'. Over a period of time I decided that the book wouldn't work, but I would still think of it occasionally.

One day, I'd been discussing the book over lunch with Julia and my son, Joe. As Joe and I walked to the station afterwards I was suddenly struck by the thought that he could help me – we could do it together! Joe had just finished his studies as a musician but he'd always been interested in writing throughout his school and university education. As a boy he would write imaginatively strange and funny tales. Joe had always been a keen listener to my childhood stories of life in Yorkshire with my

brother, and he remembered some of these better than I did. Joe was very enthusiastic about the project so we started as soon as we got home and quickly realized that it could work. He would ask me questions and then record my answers. It freed me from the feeling of pretentiousness – after all I was just talking to my son about my childhood. Joe put in most of the work writing it up, partly in my words and partly in his own. He was living with me at the time, so we were able to talk about the book every day; we worked in the same room, and I was able to work on a picture book while he transformed our interviews.

A recurring discussion between us was about the title of the book. I tried to think of a theme that's been common to all the work I've done and found myself returning to my childhood. When my brother, Michael, and I were children we invented two games. The first involved throwing a ball to the top of the stairs, watching it bounce back down and catching it before it reached the ground. It was the result of countless wet afternoons in West Yorkshire; the listless alternative to more vigorous outdoor pursuits, played by two bored but competitive boys.

The second game – the Shape Game – was far more interesting. I have spoken of this simple drawing game to children all over the world, and they have made me realize that its prevalence in my own childhood was by no means unique. Children everywhere have invented their own versions of the Shape Game. It has certainly been a very important part of my career, for I have played it in every book I have ever made.

The rules are very simple: the first person draws an abstract shape; the second person, ideally using a different coloured pen, transforms it into something. It seems that all children love this game and are very good at it – far better than adults are. It is an unfortunate part of growing up that we lose a great deal of contact with our visual imagination. The wonder with which we look at the world diminishes, and this inhibits both our inclination to draw (most adults give up entirely) and also our ability to draw with truly unfettered creativity.

Looking back, I can see that although the Shape Game is great fun, it also has a serious aspect. Essentially, the game is about creativity itself. Every time we draw a picture, or write a story, or compose a piece of music, we are playing the Shape Game. When children ask me (and they always do) where I get my ideas from, I tell them it's from the same place that they get theirs – from things that happened to me when I was a boy, from things that happened to my own children, from other people's stories, from films, from paintings, or from dreams. Everything comes from somewhere else, and when we create something we're transforming our own experience into a picture, a book, or perhaps a piece of music. We are playing our own Shape Game.

One of the interesting aspects of working on the book has been finding out how many memories of childhood incidents influenced my work, often bringing to light events I had all but forgotten and whose significance I only now fully realize. My choice of illustrations reflects these memories, but the main intention of this book is to share my delight in the Shape Game and my passionate belief in the power of art to enrich our lives.

It seems a long time ago since those early conversations with Joe and Julia, and now the work is finished. I'd like to thank Julia – for the original inspiration, her patience and enthusiasm – and Joe, of course; without his intelligence, interest and humour the book wouldn't exist. I'd also like to thank my editor Helen Mackenzie Smith for all the help and fantastic support that she's provided, and Ness Wood, too, for the superb design of the book.

Anthony Browne

Chapter One
Growing Up

The first few years of my life were spent in my grandparents' pub in Wyke, near Bradford. The Red Lion was a rough place, frequented by rough men. There was a field at the back which was in the shadow of an enormous viaduct, and one of my earliest memories is of watching from my bedroom window as a crowd formed a circle beneath it while two drunks took off their coats (perhaps even rolled up their sleeves) and shouted at each other. There were no punches thrown, and despite my young age and the unpredictability of the angry men, I felt not afraid but rather that I was witnessing something faintly absurd. Nevertheless, there was a magnificent, gladiatorial quality about the viaduct, and it left a lasting impression on me. It is a symbol that has been resurrected several times in my books.

There were times when I would wander into the

bar, stand on a table and tell stories to amuse the customers. The stories were always about a character called Big Dumb Tackle. I have no idea where the name came from, but he was a sort of (presumably unironic) Yorkshire superhero who wore an old flat cap and could fly. Big Dumb Tackle was partly influenced by the comics I read, but his origins were equally domestic. I was fascinated by one of the pub regulars, who often asked me to hit him in the stomach as hard I could. My punches were unrewarded, for he never so much as flinched, and as he belched and laughed at my useless exertions he seemed every bit as heroic as my fictional idols.

Dad loved to draw, and for a while had been an art teacher at a school in Sheffield. He worked in the pub and drew caricatures of the regulars, capturing their boozy profiles with skill and humour. He spent hours drawing with my brother and me. He may not have known it, but he was teaching us to view drawing not only as a childish occupation but as a lifelong pursuit. It is a lesson that we have never forgotten.

Most of my pictures were of great battles: soldiers, cowboys or knights in armour, all caught in moments of ferocious conflict. At first they just looked like scenes of terrible carnage, but a closer look revealed jokes, speech bubbles and snippets of descriptive writing. I loved to use words and pictures together, and long before I considered a career in children's books (as a four-year-old, I saw my future taking place in the boxing ring rather than the studio), I was creating pictures that were

Chapter opener: *My Family*, new illustration for this book, 2006

Opposite: *Hansel and Gretel*, Julia MacRae Books, 1981
Above: Dad in the Red Lion, Wyke, 1950

more interesting than they first appeared.

I haven't kept any of the battle scenes, but the picture of a pair of legs (presumably mine) overleaf, is fairly typical Browne, then and now. Unlike my actual legs, these have pirates hiding in their shoes and climbing up the 'masts'. I have learned over the years that children are natural surrealists. To a child, a pair of legs has limitless possibilities; the socks and shoes are merely the least interesting starting point. I suspect that Freud would have plenty to say about the image, but I believe I had a very secure and balanced childhood!

The drawing is an advanced example of the Shape Game. I have taken an ordinary picture and, with a few *extraordinary* additions, transformed it into a story. It has changed from something purely representational into something strange, dream-like, interesting. Of course, one could say that all drawings are examples of the Shape Game. The artist looks at a face or a tree and transforms it into their interpretation of what they see. When an image is reproduced on paper it is unavoidably manipulated, personalized, 'changed into' a drawing.

Michael and I shared a bedroom in the pub, and it was transformed one day by a firm of decorators. Instead of putting up wallpaper they created a pattern of green squiggles on the walls with their brushes. I thought this was wonderful, and I suppose those men were the Michelangelos of my early childhood. I was a nervous little boy, and sleep was impossible until the wardrobe and the space under the bed had been thoroughly checked. But somehow the green squiggles did not disturb me at all; I drifted off playing the Shape Game in my head with every one of them.

Dad had joined up when the war broke out and fought with the King's Own Yorkshire Light Infantry in North Africa. While Mum was giving birth to her first child, Jacqueline, who died when she was three days old, Dad was wounded, missing and presumed dead. It must have been a terrible time for her. Dad was recovered some days later, and because he had led patrols behind enemy lines, he was awarded the Military Cross. He had to collect the medal from Buckingham Palace, and the photograph of him overleaf alongside his mother (and mine) seems to

sum up their relationship. There was no reason for her to be there – none of the other soldiers brought their mothers – but she was a very domineering woman who was omnipresent in Dad's life. This could be quite difficult for his wife. My grandmother, like my mother, was christened Doris, but Michael and I called her Grindle. Mum disliked the name Doris, and by showing us this weakness she made sure we constantly reminded her of it. For most of her life we affectionately called her 'Our Doris'.

One of Dad's hobbies was amateur dramatics, and every year he produced a pantomime with the Brighouse Amateur Dramatics Society. I enjoyed watching the pantomimes, but found certain aspects a little frightening. I was particularly disturbed by the dames: grown men dressed in ridiculous women's clothing. Their manic attempts to be child-like made them appear mad and unpredictable as they imposed their awful jokes on

Opposite: *Silly Billy*, Walker Books, 2006
Above: childhood drawing, 1952
Right: letter to my father, c.1950s

dear dady I hope you
are feeling ~~whe~~ Well
I ~~have~~ am enJoying
my SelF. I have
JUSt Been Droring
a Scotsman. I
have not finiShs
It. I Droo a nuther
But his Body waS
to Long. Sowe I had
got to Droring
Phis ~~won~~ one theat
one ~~theat~~ theat
I am SPeaking
a-Bout. Wot I waS
torking giv my Love
to na-na ~~and~~ and Ee
Love from Tony

the strangely appreciative crowd. But my fear was somewhat counteracted by my infatuation with the Principal Boy. As I gazed from the front row, I was convinced that Joyce Hodgson – a glorious picture of espresso hair, towering legs and curious bulges – not only returned my gaze, but slapped her thighs and hooked her braces solely for me. I was only four years old, so there cannot have been any sexuality involved, yet I distinctly remember it being the

womanliness of her charms that attracted me.

My parents must have been aware of the crush because they made a point of bringing me downstairs from my bedroom one night to meet the cast. Whatever whirlwind of new emotions I expected failed to prepare me for my disappointment as, instead of the vision of loveliness I had imagined, 'Joyce' was brought before me. In reality, Joyce Hodgson was just like a lot of my parents' friends: motherly and slightly red in the face. I was disappointed, but also embarrassed as I realized what my dressing gown and pyjamas somehow confirmed me to be: a silly little bedtime boy. Looking back I can see that I felt cheated by Joyce Hodgson's Shape Game. On stage she was the very embodiment of my imaginary goddess; in my parents' kitchen she revealed the ordinary shape that was beneath the façade.

Dad occasionally performed in the pantomimes, and brought to the stage an array of skills. Certainly the highlight of *Robinson Crusoe* was the Native Chief's powerful rendition of 'That Old Black Magic', for which Dad pounded the bongo drums to accompany his own capable baritone. He could really sing. For a while he was the singer and drummer for a jazz band in Sheffield, and they made a few amateur recordings that were excellent. It was thrilling to see him in this setting: the unpredictable, dangerous tribesman threatening the white intruders with a syncopated assault. But my pride was mixed with embarrassment: the blacked-up face, the grass skirt and (most agonizing of all) the tan-coloured body stocking were far from intimidating.

My idolization of my father suffered another blow during a local variety show. A conjurer required a member of the audience to assist him on stage. Since no one else was prepared to volunteer, Dad, pitying the struggling magician, gallantly strode up to the platform. I was proud of his courage. As soon as he mounted the stage, however,

Opposite: my parents and Grindle, c. 1950s
Above, top: *King Kong*, Julia MacRae Books, 1994
Above: winning competition entry for BBC TV's
Stop, Look, Listen, 1959

it became clear that all he had done was cast himself in the role of the fool. The conjurer proceeded to play a series of tricks and jokes behind Dad's back, and as the audience laughed (moronically, I thought) at the stooge's obliviousness to the showman's 'cunning', I felt the combination of pride and embarrassment that seemed to be the staple of my childhood.

When I became a father, I learned how difficult it is to risk breaking your children's trust, whilst maintaining the social lie that is Father Christmas. My parents managed to keep up the pretence until I was about six years old, before Dad emphatically gave the game away. It was the week leading up to Christmas. I had been put to bed, and Mum and Dad saw this as an opportunity to crack on with wrapping the presents. For some reason I left my bedroom, only to discover 'Father Christmas' in his lesser-known casual attire transferring a pile of presents from one room to another. One gift, clearly marked 'Tony', was more or less spherical, a little larger than Dad's head and firm in his grasp. But any scrap of ambiguity onto which Dad might have been hoping to cling was abolished when, in his panic, he dropped the object, which duly bounced towards me. I knew everything in that moment.

Dad didn't have much luck with Christmas presents. One year I found the most incredible U.S. cavalry fort under my parents' bed. It was a large rectangular structure, complete with log walls, barracks, sleeping quarters, offices, general stores and roughly-hewn wooden ladders that led up to the top of the fort where the fighters could shoot down on the advancing enemy. Although it was brilliantly constructed, it wasn't quite finished, and there was a robust, homemade feel about the fort; it was obvious that it had been lovingly crafted by Dad's own hands. It was the perfect present.

The discovery was made several weeks prior to Christmas, so it was all I could do to keep my mouth shut in the meantime and be ready to act surprised on the big day. I still get a hot rush of anguish when I remember what happened next.

In the barn next to our house there was a higher level where Michael and I would often play and swing on the ropes that hung from the roof. To reach this level we would climb up one of several wooden ladders that were positioned along the edge of the barn. One day, apropos of nothing, I said to my parents, 'You know the wooden ladders in the barn? They look just like the kind of ladders you find in a cavalry fort!'

Why, oh why did I say it? I've been wrestling with this terrible aberration for years. I don't think I wanted Dad to know I had discovered his masterpiece. I suppose I was trying to assure him of the present's suitability by revealing, in advance of

Christmas Day, that cavalry forts were already a pre-occupation of mine. I thought he'd be pleased. But he was an adult, with an adult's sense of awareness, and of course he knew exactly what had happened. I knew this as soon as I had said it, and for the next few weeks I was tormented by regret. When Christmas Day finally came, my performance was marred by guilt, and the joy I expressed on seeing the fort for supposedly the first time must have appeared horribly contrived.

I spoke of the incident to my mother years later and she did little to ease my remorse. She told me that after the ladders comment Dad wasn't able to maintain the same enthusiasm for the completion of the project. I was mortified.

Michael started school two years before I did, and one of the highlights of my day was going with my father to pick him up in the afternoon. To mark the occasion, I would dress up as a different character each time. I don't suppose Michael was amused for one minute. I know that he and I obsessed over whichever generic characters we had encountered most recently on the big screen, and were to be seen decked out as cowboys, soldiers or pirates, according to the current craze.

We left my grandparents' pub when I was five and moved into a rented house in Lightcliffe near Halifax. Dad got a job that he hated, working for a friend selling light machinery. Mum was delighted to break free of the pub, and free of her mother-in-law.

I went to the same primary school as Michael. It was a small, cheap, but pretentious private school in

Left: *The Tunnel*, Julia MacRae Books, 1989
Above: Michael and me with our dog Major, 1951

Lightcliffe, which taught Latin to its bemused five-year-olds. Dad was a Conservative-voter who had taught at private schools himself, and considered it his duty to provide his sons with this modest privilege. Despite its shortcomings – even though there were nearly two years between us, lack of staff and teaching space meant that Michael and I were in the same class – the school was convinced it was superior to its local Church of England rival. Even Dad came to realize that this wasn't the case, for after

Above, top: image from *Man is an Animal* project, 1967
Above: *Willy the Champ*, Julia MacRae Books, 1985
Opposite, left to right: *The Tunnel*, Julia MacRae Books, 1989;
Look What I've Got! Julia MacRae Books, 1980;
The Visitors Who Came to Stay, Hamish Hamilton Children's Books, 1984

just a year he transferred both of us to the state school.

We had survived several encounters with the state school boys while we were still in private education. The route to and from our school took us past theirs, and they would take exception to our apparent airs by bumping us off the pavement, driving their bony shoulders into our blazer-bearing torsos with unconscious political intent.

The invasion of the two 'posh boys' on the first day of our transfer was met with relish by the old-timers, and I inevitably got into a fight during the first break time. As a crowd gathered, we tacitly settled into a kind of wrestle, culminating in me reproducing the only move that was ever moderately effective against my older brother: grabbing my opponent's neck under my arm and performing an act of mock-strangulation. A member of staff eventually caught us in this position and we were sent to the headmaster immediately. I felt chastened at being in trouble on the first day, but also a little aggrieved at the case of mistaken identity. What the other boy had failed to realize was that I had been merely dressing up as a posh boy the previous year.

Because we were so close in age and both enjoyed the same activities, Michael and I were best friends. We spent nearly all our time together, usually kicking, throwing, or hitting a ball of some sort. But occasionally we would seek a greater thrill in one of the many hazardous areas that served as our playgrounds. We never questioned the local park's appropriateness for our daily sporting needs, but if ever we craved the intoxicating scent of danger it was necessary to venture into one of the nearby fields or quarries where we could stay all day, if we wanted, casually risking our lives.

We lived in a fairly middle-class part of town, but we only had to wander under the railway bridge to an area called the Lydgate (pronounced 'lidjit') to find an immediate change. Suddenly the shops became cheaper, the landscape bleaker, the children rougher, the roaming dogs mangier and the potential for adventure greater.

In one of the fields, Crows Nest Park, was a well, covered by a sheet of corrugated iron. We often removed this and stared into the blackness. Experiments proved the well to be so deep that if you dropped a stone, you never heard it reach the bottom – and, as a young boy, I accepted the possibility that it never did. About a metre down the well there was a tunnel built into the side. It was a kind of initiation test for every new boy to clasp onto the grass at the top, swing his legs down into the tunnel and then manoeuvre the rest of his body into the pitch-black hole. Once inside, the passage was so narrow that it was impossible to turn round until one had crawled on one's hands and knees a few metres to the end, where the walls widened slightly. The challenge was completed by crawling back and hauling oneself up to the surface, legs dangling above the drop.

Before the eyes of other boys, Michael and I completed this challenge out of our sense of perceived necessity, but it was only several decades later that we finally admitted to each other how terrified we had been.

Our Doris never knew about these activities. She was a very warm, loving, generous woman, but she was overprotected by men throughout her life: firstly by her father, then by her husband and finally by Michael and me. Perhaps her dependence on other people contributed towards her tremendous capacity for worry.

Both my parents were readers but I don't remember many children's books being present during my early childhood. Comic annuals such as the *Beano* and *Dandy* stand out in the memory, as

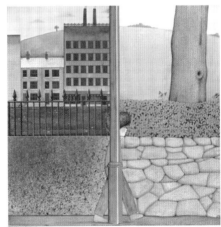

does the odd collection of fairy tales, but picture books were never really part of my upbringing. We did have a copy of *Alice's Adventures in Wonderland*, with the original Tenniel illustrations, and although I found the grotesqueness of the subjects a little frightening, it was the brilliant line drawings that drew me to the book. My understanding of the plot was nebulous at best, yet this hazy impression somehow improved the wonderland experience. As my head swam with the heady cocktail of murderous queens, talking caterpillars and mad hatters (still a terrifying partnership of words), I found Tenniel's illustrations did not clarify but rather enhanced the wonderful mysteriousness of the story.

We occasionally travelled across the Pennines to visit my cousins in Lancashire. They owned a copy of *Treasure Island* with illustrations by N. C. Wyeth. These illustrations are genuine works of art: huge, magnificent oil paintings that depict Stevenson's story with similar skill, power and dedication that the Old Masters brought to the Bible or Greek myths. Some of the images were brutal, but my fear was allayed by the knowledge that I could close the book whenever I wanted.

Although my competitive rugby days began at secondary school, my earliest memories of the game are of playing with my brother and his mates when I was nine years old. Michael had already fallen in love with the sport, and his enthusiasm helped to entice twenty-eight of his schoolmates to play regular, unofficial matches in the local park. His charitable invitation to his younger brother made it a

complete fifteen-a-side affair.

I loved everything about these games. The physical aspect came easily to me, and although I must have felt some sense of trepidation the first time I had to halt a galloping eleven-year-old flanker, the adrenaline carried me through, and before long I believed that I could tackle anybody without fear. I was by far the smallest player on the field, but I soon learned that with the right technique and plenty of intent, even the biggest lads could be brought down. The combative element was always evident to me, and it was immensely liberating to be knocking larger boys to the floor, knowing that such a mismatch in the playground would be laughable.

When I did start secondary school (Whitcliffe Mount Grammar School in Cleckheaton), the first rugby lesson could easily have caused me to revise my enthusiasm for the game. We were being taught how to tackle. I awaited my turn with relish but,

when it came, I mistimed my tackle and got my arm caught between the scissors of the ball-carrier's legs. The PE teacher thought that the best way to toughen the boys up was to laugh such incidents off as quickly as possible.

'What's the matter, lad?' he said. 'You haven't broken your arm have you?'

Determined to make a good early impression, it was a while before I admitted that yes, I certainly had.

But I continued to play all through school and into adulthood. I was captain of the school side throughout, and we were awful. I played scrum-half behind a pack of forwards that was always out-muscled, so I spent entire games just tackling.

I was born with only one pectoral muscle, and in order to protect the vulnerable left side of my

Opposite: *Alice's Adventures in Wonderland*, Sir John Tenniel, 1866
Above: *The Tunnel*, Julia MacRae Books, 1989

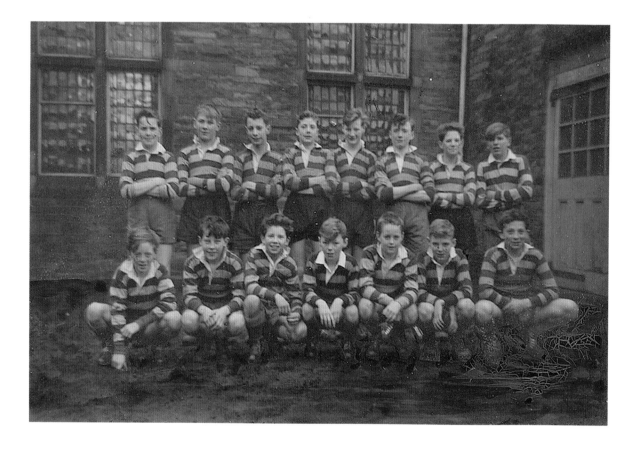

torso, Dad sewed some folded blankets into my school rugby shirt. It was typical of him. He was a fine rugby player himself, as well as a boxer, and he loved the fact that his sons enjoyed contact sports. But although he never tired of encouraging us to express our physicality and aggression, underneath the macho exterior was the most sensitive and devoted of fathers, who didn't want to see his boys get hurt.

My passion for rugby has survived throughout my life, and I still find the image of the rugby posts mildly thrilling. The distinctive capital H symbol is as instantly recognizable to me as the Christian cross is to some, or the McDonald's M is to others.

As much as I love rugby, however, the game also has terrible associations for me. Dad's heart was damaged by rheumatic fever as a boy, and exacerbated by a second bout during the war, but the severity of his condition never occurred to me when I was growing up. I was fourteen the first time I realized it was a serious concern. Michael had been due to play in a school First XV fixture, but there had been a lot of rain and the game was in danger of being cancelled due to a waterlogged pitch. Dad, who loved to watch us play and was determined that the game should go ahead, decided to take matters into his own hands: he took a garden fork to the school pitch and spent a couple of hours disturbing its surface in an effort to speed up the draining process. Our Doris went with him, and became very worried when he started complaining of pains in his chest. He remained in appalling pain throughout the drive

home, prompting Our Doris to call an ambulance as soon as they arrived. He was diagnosed with coronary thrombosis and taken straight to hospital. I arrived home from school just as two ambulance men were carrying him down the stairs in a chair (the curve of the stairs wouldn't accommodate a stretcher), and I remember him looking rather pathetic in his dressing gown. For the first time ever, I saw this God-like figure – the boxer, the drummer, the Native Chief – looking like a sick, frail old man.

Dad had another heart attack as soon as he got to hospital and subsequently had to stay there for several weeks. The first time we went to visit him in the ward I was again struck by his frailty. I saw him from a distance as we approached his bed, sitting up and looking around hopefully for his family. He looked lost. His hair was unkempt and his expression showed worry, sadness and fear: emotions that I didn't know he was capable of.

In time he recovered, but there was still clearly cause for serious concern. The heart attacks should have been a massive warning sign to me, and yet the thought of him dying seemed impossible. I was fourteen, but perhaps I wanted to hold on to the childish delusion that my parents were immortal. Dad's job involved quite a lot of travelling, and sometimes he would be late home in the evenings, turning Our Doris and Michael into gibbering heaps. They were worried that he might have died

Opposite, top: image from It's a game, like ...
only a game, *art college project, 1966*
Opposite, bottom: bottom row, third from left,
Whitcliffe Mount Grammar School Under-14's, 1959

in a car accident, but I never shared their concern because the idea was so utterly unimaginable to me. While I never had any difficulty finding other things to worry about in the middle of the night, the thought of Dad dying was something I shut out of my mind completely. It was too devastating an event to actually happen.

Rugby was easily my favourite sport, but I also represented the school at cricket and, on one memorable occasion, athletics. My short stature meant that I was less suited to short distances than some of the giants in my year, but I did develop a strategy for running the mile. Knowing my limitations as a late sprinter, I would hare off as fast as I could as soon as the starting pistol was fired. Thus, I would escape the rest of the field early on and rely on my fitness to sustain this pace throughout, hoping that the others would fail to catch up.

The day of the inter-schools athletics meeting came, and as I sized up my towering opponents, I knew I had to employ my usual tactic. The race went like a dream, and when the bell sounded for the final lap there was a fair distance between me and the other runners. But as I cruised to my apparent victory, the bell sounded again. Why? Had the bell ringer been overcome by a spontaneous desire to sound a fanfare to my glory? I looked, perplexed, at the waving arms of the race officials. What was going on? In my exhaustion I struggled to interpret their gestures, but eventually it became clear that they wanted me to run another lap! The first bell had been a mistake, and rather than

breaking the world record for the fastest mile ever covered by a human being, I had in fact run only three quarters of the race. Exhausted and a little stunned, the real final lap saw me overtaken by most, if not all of the other boys.

The local paper reported on the event, and the headline is indelibly printed on my memory: 'Boy runner broke record – then came the shocks'.

Sport dominated my childhood. When we weren't involved in organized sport, Michael and I improvised our own contests in the garden. We made a boxing ring out of cricket stumps and the washing line, and invited other boys over to challenge. But none of them were very interested, and Michael and I usually ended up fighting each other.

My strategy was all-out attack. I charged at Michael as soon as the bell rang, my head down and my arms a blur of punches, but the few that landed had little impact, and all Michael had to do was wait for an opportune moment to knock me down with a single clout.

I always thought that Michael was a lot better at sports than me, and for much of our childhood I assumed that there was no athletic feat he couldn't achieve. But I remember the moment when he first betrayed his fallibility.

Every year there was a swimming gala held at the local swimming baths. Michael hadn't been swimming long, so he was entered in the beginners' race for boys who had only achieved their initial swimming certificate. This meant that Michael's two opponents were a year younger than him. Although

Boy runner broke record — then came the shocks

Left: third from right, Halifax Evening Courier, c.1961
Below: *Willy the Champ*, Julia MacRae Books, 1985

I was mildly embarrassed by this, I had faith that Michael would prove the idiocy of the placing by thrashing the other boys into obscurity.

But from the start of the race I knew that something was wrong: Superman had lost his cape. The starting pistol was fired and Michael's opponents dived into the pool headfirst. Of course they did. That was how a swimming race always started. Everyone knew that. But the dive wasn't yet within Michael's aquatic repertoire, and he plunged gracelessly into the pool, feet first. Then — already way behind the younger boys, who had progressed seamlessly into a textbook front crawl — he resorted to the only stroke he knew: the breaststroke. He was hopeless. The other boys glided farther and farther ahead. Eventually, in a desperate attempt to restore some pride, he commenced his own clumsy imitation of their technique. It was a horrible, waterlogged dance of shame.

One of the most miserable aspects of my late childhood was that I wore short trousers until I was fifteen. My parents entertained the crazy notion that it was healthy to bare a boy's legs to the elements all year round; that the blotchy skin and calloused knees were symptomatic of the long-term good it was doing me. This philosophy was contradicted by Mum's insistence on not just drying, but also airing every item of clothing for almost a week in order to prevent us

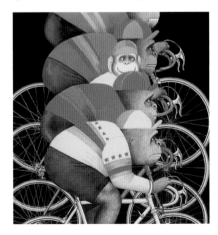

Above, top: *Willy the Wimp*, Julia MacRae Books, 1984
Above: *Willy the Champ*, Julia MacRae Books, 1985

from catching a chill. But it wasn't the functional inadequacy of the shorts that bothered me so much as the social stigma that they imposed. When I looked at the other boys in their long trousers, it seemed as if my bare legs were an indictment of my delayed entry to adulthood.

Michael was, of course, granted long trousers before me, and as I watched him parade around the house I was sure I detected in his manner more than a little peacockery. I was deeply envious. When I finally received my first pair of long trousers at fifteen (they were a hand-me-down from Michael) I was pleased of course, but the damage had already been done. I was so accustomed to the humiliation that the acceptance of the slightly tattered drainpipes seemed less like a graduation ceremony than a belated restoration of justice.

Art was my favourite subject at school. When we were allowed to draw in our own style, I was in my element, but this was rare, and there were times – even in the early years – when I was aware of a budding resentment of the way art was taught. It is a common tendency of art teachers at all levels to teach their students to work the way they do. My art teacher at school painted semi-abstract landscapes, using a four-inch brush. He objected to my careful, realistic, illustrative style at once, and on one occasion responded by making me bottom of the class.

I wanted to do art, English and biology at A-level, but the school frowned upon this combination of arts and science, so biology had to go. As a result, I had some extra free time, which I spent in the

school library looking at the art books. I wasn't aware of much public art in Yorkshire back then, and I never travelled down to London, so this was my first exposure to great paintings. It was during these periods that I discovered surrealism. The extraordinary images of Magritte and Dali were completely new to me, and yet there was a peculiar familiarity about them.

I think that most people remember one teacher who left a lasting impression. For me it is my English teacher, Frank Beckwith. He was a youngish man; dark-haired, thickset and slightly scruffy. He was bright and keen, and had acquired a vast knowledge of theatre and literature – a knowledge that was matched by his obvious passion for both. I now see that he could have been plucked straight from a black and white 1960s film about northern working-class life, probably starring Alan Bates.

It was Beckwith who introduced me to the joy of reading. His enthusiasm was infectious, and his passionately delivered lessons inspired me to pursue whatever books he recommended. Through Beckwith I discovered the plays of Samuel Beckett and Harold Pinter, and the novels of D. H. Lawrence, David Storey and Alan Sillitoe.

Beckwith was involved in local amateur dramatics, and I went with some friends to see him in *Roots* by Arnold Wesker. It was a brilliant play, he was brilliant in it, and it prompted me to seek further stimulation in the theatre. Around this time I also saw Beckett's *Waiting for Godot* and Chekhov's *Three Sisters*. I was learning to appreciate artistic expression in all its forms. It was an exciting time.

Above: *Through the Magic Mirror,*
Hamish Hamilton Children's Books, 1976
Below: *The Red Model,* René Magritte, 1936

Chapter Two
Art College

always knew that when I left school I would go to art college. Drawing and painting were my favourite things to do, and although I knew it was difficult to make a living in art, it seemed essential that I should be involved in it in some way.

I was naturally drawn towards fine art. I craved artistic freedom and dreamed of getting paid to paint whatever I liked, but I was informed enough to know that I would have to make compromises if I wanted to survive as an artist. So I chose to study graphic design at Leeds College of Art. It seemed less like a waste of time.

I'd leapfrogged a year at primary school, and left secondary school at sixteen, after just one year of sixth form, so when I started at art college I was two years younger than the other students. This difference felt enormous. They seemed so experienced and confident. Watching them swan around the college in their trendy clothes, I felt out of place and reacted by growing my hair and a beard.

For the foundation year we were encouraged to forget everything we had learned about art. If we had developed any specific skills, they were dismissed, so that all the students were starting at the same level. I was skilled with a pencil and a thin brush, so I found it excruciating to be forced to use only thick sticks of charcoal and big black brushes.

One day the tutor brought in a box of matches. He took five matches from the box and dropped them on the floor. Using charcoal sticks, we had to draw them in whichever arrangement they fell. I could understand the merit of this – the simplicity of the objects forced us to concentrate on the spatial relationships between them as opposed to the objects themselves – but I was surprised when the tutor brought the matches in again the next day

. . . and the day after that. We continued with the same exercise for three weeks!

One of the few requirements of the course that I did enjoy was life drawing. When the time came for the first class, I was still unsure of my way around the college. I couldn't find the right room. By the time I did find it I was late for the class, so I stood nervously outside the door for a while, preparing for my entrance. I pushed my way in, only to witness the most bizarre tableau. The curious details of life-drawing classes had been sniggeringly disclosed to me at school, but I was nonetheless shocked by the sight before me. There she was: a real naked woman, motionless in the middle of the room. Surrounding her were several shadowy figures. They were probably doing something no more sordid than drawing, but how could I be sure? Although I understood the nature of the class, in my giddy astonishment it seemed as if I had stumbled upon some secret perversion of academia. I hastily left the room.

Once outside, I soon realized my mistake, and went back in a few moments later, affecting an air of nonchalance. I had clearly found whatever it was I went out for! I loved life drawing because the reins were withdrawn. We were simply shown a naked body and told to draw it. It was the most freedom we were ever granted, but the tutors nonetheless emphasized that it was still an exercise, and we should view the model simply as a form for study. We were encouraged to concentrate on the physical aspects of the subject, paying attention to such

Chapter opener: painting by numbers, c.1954
Above: *Willy the Dreamer*, Walker Books, 1997
Below: Leeds College of Art poster, 1967

Graphic Design Diploma Show/Leeds College of Art/3 to 8 July/9:30 am to 6 pm each day

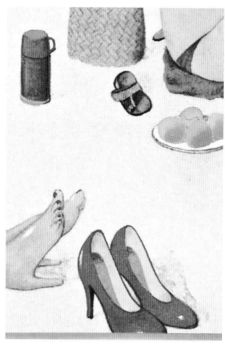

elements as form, shape, light and colour. They wanted us to draw the model exactly as we would a chair or a bowl of fruit. But I was more interested in conveying a sense of the event. I was fascinated by the extraordinary social environment we were in. The model was a conscious human being, and I couldn't help but imagine what she was thinking while we watched her.

Naked before our scrutiny, her vulnerability seemed profound. Surely it would be far more interesting if this unique atmosphere was somehow captured, as well as the mere physical aspects. As I drew, I found myself making up stories in my head about the model's life. How had she arrived in this situation? In a way, I was applying the principles of illustration to the life drawing exercise. As the course went on I became more confident, and took

more and more liberties in order to bring out the 'stories' of my life drawings. I spent a week producing a life-size painting of a female model reaching down, taking the hem of her dress and lifting it up over her head. I made several drawings depicting the different stages of the action and superimposed them on top of each other to create a sense of movement over time.

On another occasion I saw the model arrive and noticed that she was wearing a pair of red high-heeled shoes. She prepared for the class by taking everything off, but I asked her to put the shoes back on. She did, and something remarkable happened to the atmosphere. It was as if her vulnerability was suddenly evident to everyone in the room, not least to the model herself. The red shoes were almost obscenely vivid, and seemed to exaggerate rather than relieve her nakedness. The veneer of professionalism evaporated and she was suddenly exposed. She ceased to be a nude art model: she was a naked woman, willingly baring herself to a group of people. The red shoes encouraged everyone to imagine a back-story, but in a way this wasn't necessary. The real story was as extraordinary as any that we could imagine. It may sound cruel, but I found her embarrassment compelling, and I revelled in capturing the electric awkwardness of the scene.

Although I enjoyed little about the foundation year, I eventually settled into art college life and became more used to the environment. By Easter time, I was relatively content. Little did I know that Easter Monday 1964 was to be a day that would change my life and work irreparably and for ever.

It was my first year playing men's rugby with the Old Brodleians after leaving school, and I'd just been promoted to the first team for their last game of the season. It was a momentous day for the whole family, because Michael and I were to play half-backs together for the first time. It felt like a rite of passage for me, because Dad had been taking us to watch the Old Brodleians play for years, and the first-team players were my heroes. Now I was to play alongside them.

It was a beautiful, crisp spring day. The game was in the Lake District and Michael and I travelled there on the coach with the other players. It was very exciting. The game was magnificent. Michael and I impressed our teammates by playing well together

Opposite, far left: *Willy the Champ*, Julia MacRae Books, 1985
Opposite, middle: *The Visitors Who Came to Stay*, Hamish Hamilton Children's Books, 1984
Opposite, right: *Hansel and Gretel*, Julia MacRae Books, 1981
Below: art college painting from *Man is an Animal*, 1967

Referee's double trouble

GIVING a very solid performance at Bramley, the Brodleians won their second away game in succession. The 11-0 victory was well earned, for the visitors did most of the attacking.

The game was keenly contested, and a most unusual incident took place. This involved the twin brothers, Harold and David Smith.

In the first half, Harold and a Bramley player were given a severe caution by the referee. In the second half, David was involved in an incident, and the referee, under the impression he had previously cautioned him, ordered him off. When his pardonable mistake was pointed out, he allowed David to stay on.

The Brodleians gained plenty of the ball in the first half, but some tremendous covering and tackling by Bramley kept them down to a well-taken try by Walker.

After the break, Thackray cut right across to score a fine try on the left, and Mick Browne bluffed the defence to score an equally good try, which Garside converted.

Mobility

The Bramley forwards had a slight advantage in winning possession, but this was nullified by the greater mobility of the Brodleians, who responded well to the fine leadership of Wheelwright.

The tremendous tackling of the Smith brothers was a feature. The smooth harmony of the Browne brothers was also a decided asset, while all the players pulled out that bit extra when needed.

In the last line of defence, Bull had his best game yet. He fielded well and always kicked to advantage.

A repetition of the line-out work shown in the first half, plus the mobility shown in the second half, will be needed in the hard games which are scheduled for the next few weeks.

Browne brothers boost Brodleians

THE Brodleians gave a more impressive performance in beating York St. John's by 27 points to 13. The visitors are not perhaps as strong a side as they have been, yet they are fit and mobile and do not give in easily. They were 14 points down at the interval, but claimed 13 second-half points.

The decisive factor was the speed in passing and running of the Brodleian threequarters.

Some fine tries were scored.

One movement started on the Brodleian line when Tony Browne got the ball away to left winger Garside.

He raced away at top speed, Smith, (wing forward) cut across in support, took an inside pass, then drew the fullback to send Garside away to score behind the posts.

In his first senior game of the season, Garside strengthened the backs.

Successful shots

Thackray and Wilde also did well and all three scored two tries, while Radcliffe scored one, and kicked two goals from two attempts.

The pack was improved by David Smith's inclusion. He was always supporting the backs and had a hand in two tries.

Another newcomer, Tweedale, worked well in the pack, and Bull deputised capably for Young who broke a finger against West Leeds.

The Brodleians pack was second best in the line-outs, but the home men won the scrums narrowly with Cole again providing the necessary quick strike.

Walker and Wheelwright were notable performers in a pack that locked more compact than in the previous match.

The Browne brothers again organised most of the attacks. They are developing into the most competent halfback pair the Brodleians have had for quite a while.

Above, top: bottom row, third from right,
Old Brodleians First XV, 1965-1966
Above and right: newspaper cuttings, 1966
Opposite: second from left,
Old Brodleians training, c.1964

and we won the match comfortably. I had been nervous before the game, but I had come through it unscathed and triumphant. I left the field glowing with pride, looking forward to celebrating this important family triumph with my parents. Mum and Dad applauded from the touchline. The whole family was elated. Michael and I joined the other players for a drink after the game, but left fairly early, preferring to travel back in the car with our parents than return on the coach. Everything was wonderful until we got home.

Three weeks before the Easter Monday rugby match I had had what a more superstitious person would call a prophetic dream. It was simply that Dad was dead. I didn't witness the death itself: he was just dead; not there any more. I was seventeen years old, and I wasn't the most difficult of teenagers, but I had started to rebel against my parents' traditional ways. I had grown a beard and long hair, knowing that Dad would disapprove, and had developed an interest in politics that were the opposite of his.

Like most fathers of his generation, he was quite fixed in his ways, and, despite being a jazz musician himself, he objected to the exciting movements in pop music. I was enamoured of rock 'n' roll, which he considered a terrible noise compared to his Glenn Miller and Benny Goodman records, and when The Beatles arrived, he was an active participant in the general parental defence against the mania. His dismissal of modern art especially irritated me, and we had many arguments on the subject. He only liked realistic drawing and painting, and believed anything else was nonsense. As well as surrealism (which he hated) I liked Picasso, Paul Klee and Graham Sutherland, and it annoyed me that Dad couldn't overcome his prejudices to at least accept my different opinion. We argued a lot about these things. But the dream made me imagine for the first time what life would be like without him. It made me realize how much I loved him, and for the next three weeks I consciously avoided any arguments and tried hard to be more tolerant of his views. It worked. During this period we got on much better. It is comforting for me now to think that my relationship with him for those three weeks was as good as it ever was.

We arrived home from the Lake District in high spirits, and the fact that Dad couldn't get one of the electrical plugs in the living room to work wasn't going to spoil them. What happened next did. Michael and I were in the living room with Dad. Our Doris was in the kitchen. Dad was sitting in a chair, fiddling with the faulty plug when, slowly, it seemed, he fell off his chair and started writhing around on the floor. He was making the most peculiar noises. I remember the fall as like a dream:

not quite real and as if in slow motion. My first thought was that it was another of his perform-ances to make us laugh, but then I knew that such a cruel, misjudged joke wasn't in his character. It soon dawned on us that something truly terrible was happening, yet the absurd noises and exagger-ated thrashing continued to give the episode an incongruously comic, theatrical quality. It was Dad's final pantomime. Soon, like a clichéd Hollywood death scene, he began frothing at the mouth. It was absolutely horrific.

Amidst the horror, Michael and I were vaguely aware of Our Doris trying to enter the room. We didn't want her to see what was happening, and we did our best to keep her out, but she eventually forced her way past us and sank to her husband's

side. While one of us called an ambulance, she tried to perform hopeless, uneducated resuscitation procedures. She had no idea what she was doing. She pounded on his chest and thrust her mouth to his cluelessly, mimicking the histrionic gestures of TV doctors. She was desperate.

He took twenty minutes to die. Eventually the convulsing stopped and he just lay there looking dreadful. His face had turned purple, his mouth was blue and his body – though probably not actually bloated – seemed somehow enlarged in its final motionlessness. He was undeniably dead.

No reaction seemed natural. I thumped the wall repeatedly with my fist. It seemed as intelligent a thing to do as any. It was as if some evil force had entered our home and destroyed the most precious

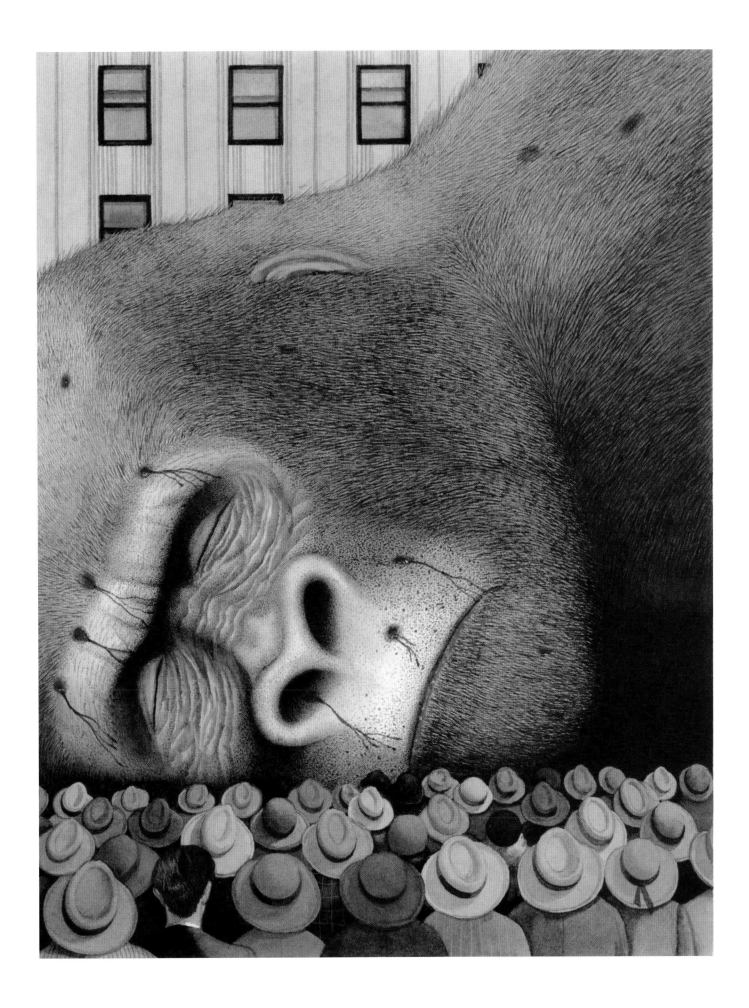

thing within it. We were forced to watch while the man we had looked to for protection and guidance all our lives – the King of the Castle, the Man of Steel – was simply wiped out. There was nothing we could do against the invisible Kryptonite. We all knew there and then that our lives had been changed forever.

The ambulance eventually arrived and he was pronounced dead on the spot. But the undertakers didn't come until the next day, and it was very difficult to sleep that night, knowing that Dad's body was downstairs.

One of the first things I did in the next few days was get my hair cut. Although I had tried to please Dad since the dream, I hadn't been prepared to lose my long hair for the sake of a little extra father-son harmony, but suddenly I was desperate to earn his approval. I had my hair cut short for the funeral in the hope that I would at least look more like the kind of son I thought he had wanted. I was in a state of shock for a long time. Soon after the funeral I had to attend a kind of trial day at the art college before they would allow me to progress from the foundation year to the graphic design course. Apparently all the prospective students had to design and make something and then attend an interview. But when I got home in the evening I couldn't remember a single detail. My mind wasn't working properly. It had blanked the event out completely.

By the time I started the course I had regained some control of my senses, but Dad's death continued to influence everything I did. I became fascinated with the human body and developed a passion for the paintings of Francis Bacon. It seemed to me that Bacon exposed our bodies as the pieces of meat they really are: a chaotic assimilation of chunks of flesh. Dad's death had made me think about the fragility of the human body. I became quite existential, and everything seemed purposeless for a while. Bacon denied the body any sense of sacredness or romanticism, and his grotesque paintings seemed to illustrate what was happening in my mind.

My interest in Francis Bacon quickly developed into an obsession with death, disease and morbidity.

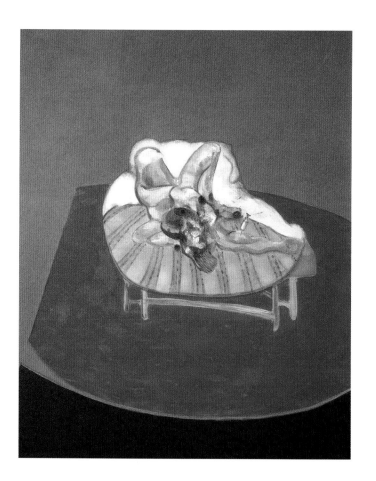

There was a museum of pathology in Leeds that I began to frequent. Among the grisly exhibits were photographs of people who had hanged themselves and unborn foetuses preserved in formaldehyde. I took my pencil with me and made drawings of the horrors on display.

Every piece of artwork I produced was infused with darkness, which was, of course, deeply inappropriate in the context of graphic design. One of the few illustration projects was to illustrate the first three letters of an alphabet book. I got very bogged down in the project, and by the end of the three-week period I had only managed to produce one illustration. It was a large, black capital 'A' on a white background. Underneath the bridge of the 'A' was the main part of the picture. Painted in gouache, it retained Bacon's lurid, fleshy tones in its depiction of a single bed in a vacant room. A bare light bulb illuminated the scene, revealing an unspecified medical instrument on the bed. The sheets were rumpled, recently disturbed, and in the middle was a dark stain. Underneath, in small lettering, the text read 'A . . . is for abortion'. It didn't go down at all well with the tutors and I was lucky not to be thrown off the course.

As time went by, the influence of death receded a little, but I always resisted the ethos of the course. It was graphic design, so a lot of the work was geared towards advertising, in which I had no interest. Ultimately I was annoyed with my decision to choose graphic design instead of fine art, but this regret took the form of resentment against the commercially orientated assignments. I would deliberately misinterpret the project briefs, handing in works of fine art that were unashamedly devoid of commercial purpose.

The feelings of social inadequacy that I experienced when I first started at the college vanished fairly quickly, and instead I began to view the other graphic design students as part of the regime against which I rebelled. Whereas (I thought) they dressed like graphic designers, I made a point of dressing like a fine art student – or, at least, how I imagined a fine art student dressed. This wasn't easy in 1960s Yorkshire. Most of the men's clothes were very boring, and it took an inspired shopper to achieve a look that was distinctive. But I had a few ideas up my frilly sleeve. I bought some ice-skating boots and sawed the blades off to make them into a pair of almost serviceable shoes, and I gave my own jacket design to a tailor, which he dutifully converted into an extraordinary garment. It was covered in buttons and must have looked ridiculous, but I was delighted with it. It was different!

Throughout my time at art college I never once considered a future in children's books. Apart from the alphabet book, I can remember one other illustration project that was directly related to what I do now. The brief was simply to write and illustrate a children's picture book. The fact that we were given

Previous spread: *King Kong*, Julia MacRae Books, 1994

Opposite: *Lying Figure with Hypodermic Syringe*, Francis Bacon, 1963

only a month to complete it seems even more non-sensical to me now than it did then. I didn't enjoy the project at all. I formed a story around some observations I had made while taking my mother's dog for a walk. It was about a man and a woman – strangers to each other – who take their dogs for a walk in the same park. While the dogs play together joyously, their owners sit on the bench in silence, refusing to so much as look at each other. It didn't seem much of a story (I had no idea that I would revisit it twice with *A Walk in the Park* and *Voices in the Park*), and I had little enthusiasm for the project. I resented the short amount of time that we had to complete it, and I had great difficulty drawing the dogs. I tried to make them look like cartoon, child-friendly dogs – benign and playful – yet somehow the influences of death and Francis Bacon showed through, resulting in the creation of hellish, big-eyed monsters that would have terrified even the bravest of children.

I may not have considered writing children's literature at this stage, but I did spend a lot of time making books at art college. Much of the course was taken up with typography, designing logos for nonexistent firms, and other design-based projects that failed to engage me, but at last I became enthused when the college bought a ring-binding machine. Although it didn't exactly produce books, it allowed me to join pictures together to form a book-like layout. I used it all the time. The first 'book' that I produced was about the human heart. It was full of images of the heart, including text-

book-like studies and diagrams, realistic drawings and surrealist paintings. I had made series of pictures before, but there was something especially exciting about actually combining the pictures within two covers and turning the pages to get a true sense of progression through the series.

One of my proudest accomplishments was a book about rugby: It's *a game, like . . . only a game.*

I carried on playing rugby for the Old Brodleians after Dad's death and throughout college, but my daily life as an art student always made it feel like a guilty pleasure. I looked like an art student with my long hair and arty clothes, and in many ways I felt

Above and opposite: images from *It's a game, like . . . only a game*, 1966

like one, even in the presence of the rugby players who conformed to the mainstream fashions of the times and must have thought how odd I looked in their dressing room. But I loved rugby, and when I was on the pitch it felt very natural to me. In truth I felt slightly uncomfortable in both environments. I was good at art and quite good at being 'arty', but there was something about the lifestyle that I found tiresome and pretentious, and whereas I loved playing the game itself, many aspects of rugby culture repelled me. The baying crowd, the relentless machismo, the excessive booze, the dirty songs and the horseplay were not to my taste. But unbeknown to most of my fellow students I continued to play rugby every Saturday afternoon.

I think the rugby book conveys my ambivalence

about the game quite well. It incorporates a variety of different styles, and the images demonstrate a mixture of affection and contempt for the game. It also foreshadows my future in picture books, for much of its impact comes from the relationship between the words and the pictures.

There was one tutor at art college whom I really respected. Derek Hyatt was a painter as opposed to a graphic designer, and I think he felt miscast as a teacher on the course in the same way as I did as a student. Based on our mutual alienation, an affinity developed between us that seemed to make him more tolerant of my work than the other tutors were. Like Frank Beckwith at school, he was the one tutor whom I found genuinely inspiring. Hyatt taught me a memorable lesson: to treat art as a form of communication. This lesson has been vital to me,

for even though I use words to accompany my illustrations, I always try to make the pictures tell much of the story, and communicate things that the words do not.

It was Hyatt who came up with the idea for my last degree project. The effects of Dad's death were still powerful, and I continued to entertain existential thoughts. I became interested in the relationship between animal and human behaviour. I was convinced that, for all our consciousness and logic, our decisions are dictated by our bestial instincts.

Hyatt knew about this interest. He encouraged me to research the subject and create a piece of artwork based on my findings. The result was my degree exhibition, 'Man is an Animal'. The exhibition consisted of four large oil paintings and a book.

 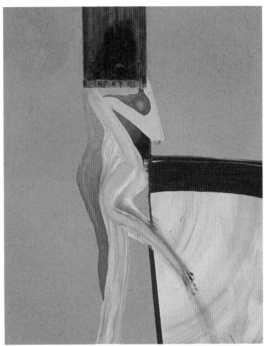

The pictures in the book were of people indulging in typical everyday activities, but the accompanying text for each image described basic animal behaviour. It related to the picture books that I make now, in which the relationship between the words and the pictures is rarely uncomplicated. I like to include differences and gaps between the two components that the reader has to fill in with his or her imagination.

With the *Man is an Animal* book, I was trying to illustrate the similarities between human and animal behaviour. For the final show I put the book on a table and surrounded it with the four Baconesque oil paintings. They were large, figurative canvases – untitled, but with vague themes such as aggression and sexuality. The paintings were intended to imply the connection between human and animal behaviour, without spelling the message out as the book did. I thought the display was good, but when the assessor came to mark my degree, his comment on the final project was that it wasn't graphic design and he therefore couldn't give it a mark. I disagreed, but I wasn't totally surprised.

Opposite, left: 'The expression of the male social bond is in the doing of certain things together, e.g. hunting' from *Man is an Animal*, 1967

Opposite, right: 'Bird songs advertise the sex and species of the singer, and serve as long range attractors to the opposite sex' from *Man is an Animal*, 1967

Above: images from *Man is an Animal*, 1967

Chapter Three

Bodies and Greetings Cards

The one thing I was fairly clear about when I left college was that I wanted to be a painter and not a graphic designer. But I had to make some money in the meantime, so I applied to do a teacher training course at Goldsmiths College in London. Somebody had told me that the Goldsmiths course was quite free and that trainee art teachers were encouraged to develop their own artwork as part of the course. It sounded perfect: I could carry on painting, while still doing something 'useful'.

Just one morning at the college was enough for me to change my mind. It seemed to be a lot more regimented than I had expected, with a far greater emphasis on the teaching than the art. I had been naive and was on the course for the wrong reasons, so, after literally one morning, I trudged back to Yorkshire, devoid of plans.

I moved back home with Our Doris. By this time Michael had moved to Kent to take up a teaching position in a girls' grammar school, so it was me, Our Doris, Grindle (who had moved in after my father died) and a couple of lodgers. It was a grim environment. I longed to get a job as soon as possible, just so I had somewhere to go, but I had to endure a period of unemployment. Thankfully, my good friend from art college, John Rowley, was in the same position, and we tried to evade the doldrums by setting each other illustration projects. This kept me painting at least, but it did nothing to fill my pockets. I still hoped to find the elusive profession that combined my skills and interests.

My search took me to the careers section of the local library. There was little of relevance, and (in the absence of an implied partner publication) I found myself flicking surreptitiously through

Careers for Girls. To my astonishment, I found what seemed to be the perfect job. Medical illustration involved making small, detailed illustrations of operations to be used in medical journals and text-books. I could hardly believe it. It was a job that simultaneously satisfied my need to paint and my fascination with the insides of people's bodies. The influence of Francis Bacon could not have been more professionally applicable!

I did some research and found out that St Bartholomew's Hospital in London ran a medical illustration course every two years. They accepted only four students for each new intake, but this didn't curb my enthusiasm. I went back to my old school and got a preserved rat from the biology department. I dissected it and made several paintings to illustrate the various stages of the dissection. A rabbit's leg and a cow's eye – courtesy of the local butcher – got the same treatment, and I made some diagrammatic drawings of the heart and circulatory system to complete what I thought of as an impressive portfolio.

I applied for the course and was offered an interview. I took it very seriously. I didn't want to satisfy any prejudices they might have about my generation, so I got a haircut and wore a suit and tie for the occasion. I was confident. Not only was my portfolio good, but my desire for the position would surely impress the panel.

The interview seemed to go well. I toned down my northern accent and presented myself as polite, keen and articulate. But I was surprised to get a

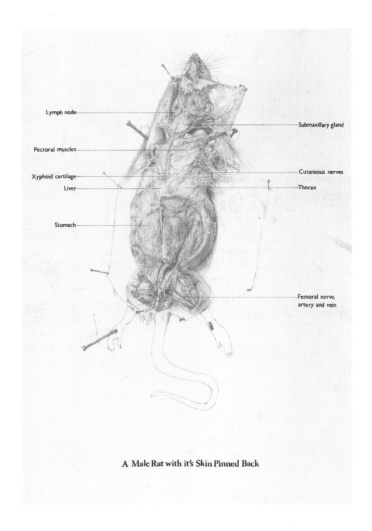

A Male Rat with it's Skin Pinned Back

Chapter opener: Valentine's card for Gordon Fraser, c.1980

Above: dissected rat, c.1968

letter a few days later to say that I had not been accepted on the course. I was very disappointed.

Just as I was preparing for another indefinite spell in the mire, however, I received another letter. It was from one of the men on the interview panel. He said he was sorry I had not been accepted on the course, but he wanted to make me aware that there was a job available as assistant medical illustrator at

Manchester Royal Infirmary. I was very grateful to him, and I applied for the job at once.

I was offered another interview. This time the panel was made up of surgeons and university professors as opposed to medical illustrators, and they were under the illusion that art students spent a lot of time studying anatomy. I knew better, but decided it was best not to contradict them. I gladly accepted the job.

I was employed by Manchester University to produce illustrations to help the medical students understand the operations. I was on the same pay rate as the university lecturers, and it seemed like fantastic money, but I was also terrified. I hadn't a clue what I was doing and I had to learn everything on the job. It was incredibly difficult.

A typical job was like this: a surgeon would come to me and explain that he had developed a new strategy, and he wanted me to illustrate his methods for the students. He (and it always was a he) would use the illustrations either as slides for a lecture he was giving, or to accompany an article he had written for *The British Medical Journal*.

I had to attend the operation and make a sketch of each surgical procedure. Later, in the studio, I converted the sketches into more detailed paintings. The surgeon would pause at various points throughout the operation to show me what he was doing and allow me to make a more detailed drawing. But it was almost impossible. In reality, an operation is a mess. Instruments, hands and blood get everywhere, obscuring all the details and casting a red veil of ambiguity over everything. One organ looks much like another in the vast casserole of the human body. Photographs are useless for educational purposes, which is why the university employed artists like me.

The operations were horrific to witness. The vast amount of blood was unpleasant, but worse still were the appalling things that were taken from people's bodies: huge, evil-looking tumours, glinting malignly as they were lifted from their biological lairs. But there was no time to be squeamish. I spent the whole time in a state of intense concentration, desperately trying to understand what was going on.

Occasionally, if it had been a particularly complicated procedure, the surgeon would take me down to the mortuary to review the operation on a dead body. This was the part of the job that I could barely endure. Entering the mortuary was like stepping into a Hieronymus Bosch painting. It was a huge room with row upon row of slabs, each supporting a naked corpse. The bodies were of all ages, shapes and sizes, at various stages of decay. Supine and naked on their charmless slabs, they looked completely vulnerable, and it was as close to a vision of hell as I have seen. The surgeon would take his pick from the display and open up the body to show me the procedure, releasing an ineffably foul stench that would remain in my nostrils for days afterwards. The ordeal was made worse by the horrible soundtrack: peculiar squelches, gaseous emissions and the mosquito drone of electric saws being used to cut through skulls. I never acquired

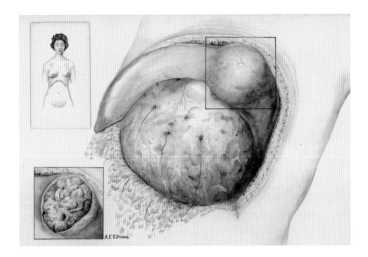

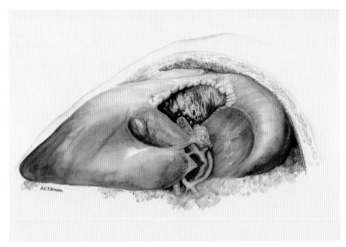

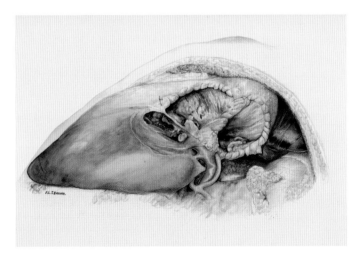

Above: sequence of illustrations from a liver operation, c.1970

a shield of professional indifference, and I was always conscious that the bodies belonged to real people. But, horrific though the mortuary was, I preferred the company of the mortician to that of many of the university lecturers, and I eventually became sufficiently used to the environment to eat my lunch occasionally with him amid the corpses.

The most interesting part of the job was the process of transforming my sketches into finished paintings. The sketches were speculative, to say the least, and it was a challenge to turn what was a veritable bloodbath into a comprehensible sequence of events. In the end, the paintings that I produced were far from honest representations of the real operations. I had to depict the organs as clear and identifiable – not the shapeless, blood-soaked objects they actually were. It was very much an imaginary, 'cleaned-up' impression of the scene. Although *Gray's Anatomy* was useful for clarifying the anatomical accuracies, the task required a lot of imagination on my part. With no reference other than the sometimes nonsensical drawings I had rapidly scrawled in the operating theatre, I had to rely on my imagination to turn the operation into a story that could be easily read. It was a difficult story to tell. Quite often something significant was obscured by an organ or the surgeon's hands or a medical instrument, and I had to guess at what happened behind the offending object. For the first time in my life, I was getting paid to play the Shape Game.

I have always said that I learned more about

drawing and painting in my two and a half years at the hospital than I did in my four years at art college. All I ever did in the job was make 'realistic' pictures, and this constant practice was hugely beneficial to my technique. I had hardly used water-colour before, but during this period I spent hours learning how to control its tricky ways, and before long it became my medium of choice. I also benefited from the fact that nobody was judging my work from an artistic standpoint. Each time I put brush to paper, it didn't matter whether I produced an attractive picture or not; it needn't be aesthetically pleasing or worthy on an artistic level. It wasn't trying to sell anything. The picture need not appeal to anybody: it was simply a practical image to serve a specific function. All artistic judgement of my work was suspended during this period, and my confidence grew as a result.

I look back on my time at Manchester Royal Infirmary as my most productive training period as an illustrator. They were the years during which I developed the skills that have served me throughout my career. Not only did I improve significantly as a draughtsman, I also learned how to tell difficult stories through a series of pictures.

As valuable as it was, the work eventually became repetitive. To make the job more interesting I started introducing hidden figures into the paintings. If you look closely at my later medical illustrations, you might see little people clambering out of an open thorax, swinging from a ribcage or peering into an ear. They were tiny, ambiguous and purely

for my own amusement (as far as I know, nobody else ever noticed them). On one level they were frivolous schoolboy doodles, but they were also the symptoms of frustration. They represented the creative part of me that wasn't being sufficiently exercised. I knew it was time to move on.

I left the hospital and again enrolled on a teacher training course, this time at Leeds. I lasted a little longer than before (three weeks!), but then decided once and for all that I didn't want to be a teacher. After a period of drifting, I bumped into a friend from art college, Clive Rand, who had started his own advertising company in Leeds. He offered me a few illustration jobs for the company. I gladly accepted the work, but hated every minute of it. As soon as I started to work I felt as if I was back at art college, with all the familiar feelings of anxiety and incompetence. I thought I was quite good at illustration, but I was awful at this.

One job I remember was to design a double-page spread for a Sunday newspaper, advertising mail order products. The firm was selling household goods such as sun-beds, bathroom cabinets and electric lawnmowers. I was given photographs of the items that showed them as they were – cheap, plastic, prosaic – and it was my job to make drawings that somehow transformed them into bright, attractive purchases. But I wasn't in the mood for the Shape Game and I drew them to look as dull as they really were. The client wasn't very happy, but published them nonetheless. I can't imagine that many people flocked to buy a new lawnmower after seeing my illustration.

Another job was to advertise caravan furniture. I was asked to draw a happy family in a caravan, laughing and smiling, every one of them ebullient in their paradise-on-wheels. But although medical illustration had largely exorcized my obsession with death, I still found it impossible to draw happy people, and even after several attempts what was intended to be an idyllic family scene looked like a prelude to something dreadful. The people were smiling, but their expressions seemed to be painted on. They knew what was coming. Try as they might to enjoy their final moments, it was only a matter of time before the starved hounds of hell descended on the flimsy caravan . . . possibly in an attempt to get at the lovely new furniture.

I did a few more of these advertising jobs, but I didn't enjoy them and the money wasn't enough to live on, so I started to look for other illustration-based work to top up my income. Greetings cards were just beginning to improve, with a few more imaginative designs creeping into the market. Jan Pienkowski had launched his firm Gallery Five, which produced graphic, comparatively trendy designs to counter the cutesy animals and syrupy verses that then dominated the shelves.

I knew very little about the market, so I designed some cards that were somewhere between these two styles, and sent them to the Gordon Fraser Gallery. Gordon Fraser was an intelligent, cultured man who produced greetings cards to support his glossy art books and the small art gallery that he ran in Cambridge. He loved art, and the cards were a commercial necessity to cover the losses that he made with the books and the gallery.

I sent him three or four designs. In the accompanying letter I explained that there were more where these had come from (there weren't), and asked if he would grant me an interview. He wrote back to say that he would like to see some more from my collection. I instantly rushed to produce them!

Gordon was a nice man who wanted to encourage me, and he bought some of my pictures even though he knew they wouldn't sell. He advised me on how I might improve them and told me to persevere, so over the next year I sent him a lot of designs, many of which he bought with no intention of publishing. Gradually I learned what interested the market. My designs got more and more saleable, until eventually Gordon Fraser was publishing most of them.

Below: various illustrations for Gordon Fraser, c.1980

It was 1971. Michael had been living in Kent for two years and was married with a baby on the way. Now that I had stopped working for the advertising agency and was starting to have some success with the greetings cards, it made sense for me to move down south where I would be closer to my brother and closer to Gordon Fraser's London offices. I got a detestable little flat in Ramsgate. It was rank and cockroach-infested. If I forgot to turn the light on when I went for a pee in the middle of the night, I trod on the little buggers with my bare feet. It made a resounding crunch.

I lived in Ramsgate for several years. It was nice to be by the sea, but it could be a depressing place at times. There wasn't a lot to do. One night while at a seedy little nightclub on the seafront, spending what little money I had earned that week on beer, I met a young violinist, Jane. She was drinking with one of her friends, and in the midst of what was a fairly shabby crowd, she was charming and interesting. We struck up a conversation and got on very well. A few years later Jane and I were married

a storm in a tea-cup

Flappy Birthday

and stayed so for twenty-five years, having two wonderful children together.

Gordon Fraser greetings cards provided my only income. I got more designs printed than most artists because I learned to vary my styles. The company couldn't afford to print too many cards that were obviously by the same artist, so I made sure that my designs were as different as possible: cartoons, realistic paintings, line drawings . . . Some were funny, some were sentimental; others were just plain dull. The intention was to make them look as if they had been produced by different artists. It was very commercial and my heart wasn't in the job much of the time, but at least the need to be diverse broadened my repertoire of skills. I became a much more versatile illustrator during this period, and although a lot of the cards make me cringe when I look at them now, I can see how they shaped my approach to children's books.

Above and opposite: various illustrations for Gordon Fraser, c.1980

Chapter Three: Bodies and Greetings Cards   55

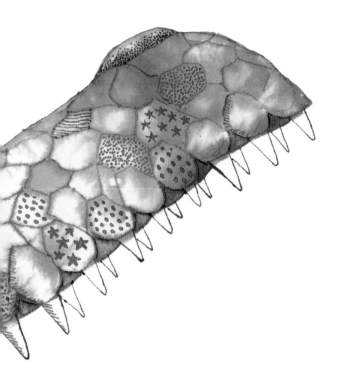

Chapter Four
First Books

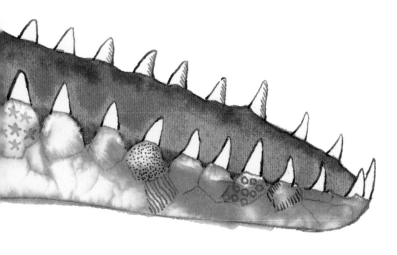

Although I was getting a lot of designs published, the greetings cards job was not well paid. I hated living in squalid conditions, so I began to consider other ways of making money. From what I had learned about the profession, the two most common follow-up jobs for former greetings card artists were in women's magazines and children's books. At that time short romantic stories were a popular feature of women's magazines, and – providing you could rustle up an attractive female patient and an improbably handsome doctor – there was work to be found. I could see myself becoming very quickly bored with this; at least children's books allowed for more variation.

I chose a selection of my card designs that seemed to suit the picture-book market and sent them to several children's book publishers. I got a few responses. One was from the editor (and legend of the children's book world) Mabel George, who offered to meet me at the impressive offices of Oxford University Press. She saw some promise in my style, and set me a trial project to illustrate a book called *Flambards* by K. M. Peyton. I was told to come back when I had produced four pictures and she would reassess my employability. The book was about a young girl and her horse. I had little interest in illustrating the story, and was bored long before I had finished. It felt like hard work, and although my black and white drawings weren't bad, they reflected my apathy for the project. It wasn't a good introduction.

As it turned out, I never had to take the *Flambards* illustrations back to Mabel George, because I was offered an interview with the art director at Hamish Hamilton, Michael Brown. He also liked my style, but instead of setting me a trial project, he suggested

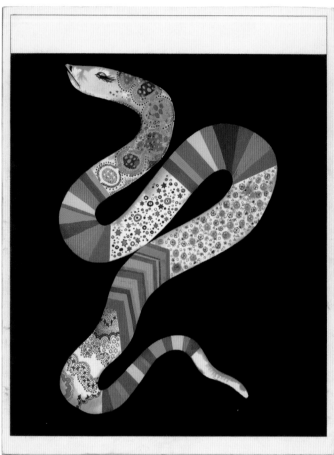

that I simply produce my own picture book. The freedom of this appealed to me, but I hadn't a clue where to start. I knew nothing about children's books. I went to the library and looked at the work of Brian Wildsmith and John Burningham, hoping to get an idea of how picture books were supposed to look.

From what I could gather, animals were perennially popular, so with Wildsmith's and Burningham's styles in mind, I developed a book about a young elephant who wanders away from his mother and gets lost in the jungle.

The elephant asks various animals if they know the way home, but none of them have the time for him. A mouse says he can help, but the elephant dismisses the offer because the mouse is too small. As more and more animals ignore him, the mouse persists, until the elephant eventually agrees to let him help. The mouse may be small, but he proves to have a heart of elephantine proportions! He climbs on the elephant's back and guides him home to his worried mother.

It wasn't a very original story and they weren't original pictures, but I hoped that the book was thematically in the right sort of area. I painted the pictures on thick watercolour card. In my naivety, I thought that it was my responsibility to 'make' the book myself, so I stuck all the pictures together to create an absurdly heavy book-like structure that was about a foot thick.

I dragged it back to Michael Brown. After politely pointing out my error, he told me he was interested in my potential, and thought that I would benefit from a discussion with Hamish Hamilton's children's book editor, Julia MacRae. In my early meetings with Julia she was very helpful in guiding me out of my ignorance, and she taught me many valuable lessons about picture books. Julia told me about dummies (rough preliminary versions of the book with sketchy drawings and words which propose the layout), and encouraged me to discuss each stage with her instead of rushing straight into the final product. Once I had been suitably coached, she thought that I had the ability to produce publishable picture books.

Julia was my official editor right up until her retirement in 1996, but she continues to advise me today. She has been a massively positive influence throughout my career. It is her enthusiasm, encouragement and, above all, her belief in my work that have given me the confidence to keep going all these years. I cannot stress enough what a comfort it is to have such a highly respected supporter as Julia MacRae. Her skills as an editor are superb. Perhaps it is her extensive knowledge of art and its history – something that is very unusual in a

Chapter opener: illustration from the *Elephant Book*, c.1974

Previous spread, opposite and above:
illustrations from the *Elephant Book*, c.1974

literary editor – that enables her to help find exactly the right words to fit the pictures.

Her editing of my books was brilliant, and she brought a fluency to the text that I could not have accomplished alone. I know that she has a passion for music and is extremely musical herself: perhaps this is why her words have such effortless rhythm.

It was Julia who taught me a crucial lesson about picture books: to leave a gap between the words and the pictures. Rather than treat the pictures as merely a visual representation of the events described in the text, there can be something in the illustrations that the text does not reveal. Likewise, there can be something in the text that is not apparent in the illustrations, and sometimes there can be things omitted from both. The gaps are left to be filled in by the reader's imagination. Julia's lesson has been invaluable in shaping my style as a picture-book creator, and without it, there would be less of the tension between the words and the pictures that is often present in my work.

But apart from her professional guidance, Julia has always been a fine friend. It is a testament to the quality of our friendship that she is still happy to help and advise me now, even though our professional relationship has officially come to an end. I am hugely grateful to Julia for all that she has done for me.

Back in 1976, it was thanks to Julia that I got to know a lot more about picture books. But what I needed was an idea. My first thought was to draw upon 'The Door', a poem by Miroslav Holub about a mysterious closed door. The stanzas provided a variety of imaginative suggestions as to what could be behind it.

I borrowed this idea and made a picture-book dummy. On every other page was an image of a door, with the words 'Go and open the door' underneath. On the opposite page (behind the door) was a suggestion such as 'Maybe it's an invisible man' or 'Perhaps it's a dog taking a man for a walk'. Each suggestion was accompanied by a surrealist illustration. There was no story as such: it was just a book about imagination. I enjoyed painting

what was behind the doors, but, as varied as I tried to make them, the doors themselves insured that half the book was very boring. I wasn't at all convinced that the book worked, but I took the dummy to Julia for her opinion nonetheless. She agreed that the idea wasn't substantial enough as it was, but she thought that something interesting could be developed from it. She was struck by one particular illustration which showed a boy looking in a mirror and seeing the back of his head in the reflection: 'Maybe it's a magic mirror'. The image was inspired by Magritte's 'Not to Be Reproduced'. Julia suggested that I take this image as the starting point for a story in which a boy discovers a magic mirror that he is able to walk through. The strange dream world that he enters would allow me to reproduce the surreal scenarios I had developed in the book about the doors.

The result of Julia's suggestion was my first book, *Through the Magic Mirror*. The protagonist, Toby, has an uneventful home life – his parents are portrayed as either sleeping or watching the television. Desperate for adventure, Toby looks in the mirror one day and sees the back of his own head. He steps through the glass and enters a strange world. The setting is the same dull street that he has known all his life, but everything is peculiarly altered.

The book is purely a vehicle for the surrealist imagery I had devised before, and the story was developed entirely from the pictures. In other words, I drew a series of pictures first and then forged a story clumsily around the assemblage. To create the illustrations first and then write a story in response

Opposite and above: *Through the Magic Mirror*,
Hamish Hamilton Children's Books, 1976

to them is, in my opinion, the worst way of approaching a picture book. Since the naive *Through the Magic Mirror*, I have learned that the best way, for me at least, is to develop the words and pictures at the same time, constantly considering the effect that one has on the other.

In spite of my reservations about the book, Hamish Hamilton agreed to publish *Through the Magic Mirror*, and it did quite well. Julia was pleased and encouraged me to get started on another book as soon as I could. This time I decided to have a story in mind before I started the pictures, so I returned to the narrative that I had first illustrated at art college about the two people walking their dogs. I was a little tentative because I remembered how grotesque the dogs had looked in my first attempt. I hoped that the intervening years had

softened their gargoyle-like features!

I took a rough pencil dummy to Julia. She liked the idea, but thought that the absence of children in the story was ill-advised. I changed the story accordingly, and found that the addition of the children provided a sub-story that improved the book considerably.

Mrs Smith, her son Charles and their Labrador, Victoria, all go for a walk in the park. At the same time Mr Smythe, his daughter Smudge and their scruffy mongrel, Albert, embark on a parallel outing. The two parties arrive at the park, and while the dogs develop an immediate friendship and bound into exuberant play, the humans sit at opposite ends of the park bench, refusing to acknowledge each another.

Gradually, the two children edge closer together.

They eventually abandon the adults and follow the dogs' example by choosing companionship over prejudice. The children remove their overcoats (a gesture that I later decided in a television interview symbolized the removal of their social armour or opposing military uniforms) and they have a fantastic time. At the end of the story Charles picks a flower and gives it to Smudge, before being whisked home by his mother. Smudge, too, is told it is time to leave. The adults have continued to sit at opposite ends of the park bench throughout the story, oblivious to the joy around them. The final picture in the book shows the flower, which Smudge has kept in a jam jar on the window-sill.

A Walk in the Park was seen by many to be a book about class, but I really intended it to be about general human behaviour. When I had taken my mother's dog for a walk I observed all kinds of people, and most of them ignored me (perhaps due to my shaggy appearance), while our dogs gambolled and sniffed their way into the most intimate of friend-ships. There are, of course, certain customs of the canine social routine that I wouldn't willingly introduce to the human world, but their unending desire for friendship and their total

Opposite and above:
A Walk in the Park,
Hamish Hamilton Children's Books, 1977

lack of discrimination are exemplary traits. As I watched my mother's dog embody the vices and virtues of its species, I realized that the only social contribution I ever imparted at these times was the occasional mumbled apology to a fellow walker as my four-legged responsibility crossed the line between friendliness and obscenity with an unsuspecting poodle. I was as salient an example as anybody of the British tendency towards reservedness, and *A Walk in the Park* was my comment on what seems to be a widespread phenomenon. I made the two families from different class backgrounds purely to emphasize the barriers between them.

My main concern was that the story was not eventful enough for children. If I was to illustrate the events of the story exactly as they happened in the text, the pictures would simply show people walking in a park, with very little visual appeal for children to engage with. So, as I had done with the tiny figures in my medical illustrations, I found myself incorporating hidden jokes and absurdities into the pictures. At a quick glance, the images are as ordinary as I feared they would be, with as little embellishment as the simple tale they illustrate. But a closer look reveals that along-side the events in the foreground, there are all sorts of unusual goings-on in the background. While the main characters stroll through the park, the details in the background include a man taking a tomato for a walk, Robin Hood practising his archery and a woman pushing a dog in a pram. A few pages later, Father Christmas can be seen kicking a red ball while Tarzan swings through the trees above him. Painting these details kept me amused and also allowed me to continue the surrealist theme that had dominated *Through the Magic Mirror*. I hoped that if the background stories prevented me from becoming bored as I illustrated the story, they would have the same effect on children as they read it. But I didn't think about it too much at the time: it was just something I had done since childhood, as the picture of the pair of legs testifies. Shortly after *A Walk in the Park* was published, however, I was asked to appear on a BBC2 programme with Aidan Chambers, and one of the first questions he asked me was 'Why do you include hidden details in your pictures?' I was sure that he expected a more intelligent answer than, 'They're fun to draw and they make the pictures more interesting,' so I groped for a more intellectual response. I said that the hidden details reflected the way that children look at the world, because they are seeing things for the first time. Their highly tuned imaginations make even the ordinary things appear new and strange. This is exactly what the surrealists were trying to do: return to that childish state of wonder at seeing

the world for the first time. By placing ordinary objects in an unusual context, they created a dream-like world that was at once familiar and at the same time new and extraordinary. Their intention was to see these objects as if for the first time.

I wasn't thinking any of this when I made the paintings and I thought it sounded a bit pretentious when I said it, but I now believe that there was some truth in my answer to the question. With the hidden jokes and characters, I was reverting to the way in which I had drawn as a child, and I think that one of the reasons my books have been popular with children is because the illustrations reflect their outlook on the world. My interest in surrealism has helped me to stay in touch with childhood.

Chambers asked me another question that day. He wanted to know about the significance of brick walls in my books. I had absolutely no idea, and this time I told him so. It was twelve years before I painted what I considered to be my first significant brick wall!

Although my picture-book career had begun, I was still working for Gordon Fraser at this time. As well as greetings cards, the company sold wrapping paper. On one occasion Gordon asked me to create a wordless, comic-book-like story for a wrapping paper design, preferably with a catchy, child-friendly character. I came up with a little white bear who wore a bow tie and carried a magic pencil. He used the pencil to draw his way out of trouble, for every-thing he drew became real. Bear cruised across the wrapping paper drawing specific solutions to a

Right: *Bear Hunt,*
Hamish Hamilton Children's Books, 1979

variety of obstacles.

I realized that it was a suitable idea for a young children's book. Although it contradicted the free, painterly style that I enjoyed, certain influences were starting to put me in a more commercial frame of mind. After *A Walk in the Park* was published, I went to a sales conference where I received a commercial critique of my first two books. The salespeople believed my books were unlikely to sell because they were too artistic, self-indulgent and aimed at adults rather than children. One particular comment infuriated me at the time: the suggestion that I should produce books more like the Mr Men series. I had nothing against the Mr Men books; they were just clearly not my style.

I left the conference angry, but something must have registered, because the next book I made was *Bear Hunt*. Although they are nothing like the Mr Men series, the *Bear* books are the closest I have ever come to a repetitive, motif-based, series style of picture-book production.

My attempt to make my work more commercially viable is evident on the very first page of *Bear Hunt*. The style is dramatically different from that of my first two books. The illustrations take the form of boldly outlined ink drawings, and instead of

watercolours I used coloured inks to create large areas of bright, flat colour.

Unlike my previous books, *Bear Hunt* is neither realistic nor surrealistic, and I view it more as a flirtation with the comic-book style than a classic picture book. Although it departs from my usual style in many ways, I continued to include the hidden stories in the background. I thought that what the salespeople had branded the 'clever stuff' in the pictures – the stuff they thought was intended to impress adults – was vital for children's lasting enjoyment of the book. I wanted children to notice something different each time they read it.

Bear Hunt was personally relevant to my own situation. I took on board what the salespeople had suggested mainly because I was struggling for money; I was as keen as they were for my books to be financially successful. By creating the more commercial *Bear Hunt*, I borrowed Bear's own strategy of drawing my way out of my trouble. I drew to escape both my own poverty and also my reputation among the salespeople as a non-commodity. Unlike Bear, however, I possessed neither a magic pencil nor, tragically, a spotty bow tie to help my cause.

Bear Hunt did well, but it wasn't the kind of book that I wanted to make every time. As I had done with the greetings cards, I eventually learned to strike a balance in my work between commercial viability and artistic worth.

After *Bear Hunt*, I made *Look What I've Got*. In the story, Jeremy is inundated with material possessions, and he loves to show off his latest

Opposite: *Bear Hunt*, Hamish Hamilton Children's Books, 1979
Above: *Look What I've Got!*, Julia MacRae Books, 1980

acquisitions to Sam, who apparently has nothing except his highly active imagination for entertainment. It is no surprise which of them is ultimately the happiest.

My work was steadily improving, but it wasn't until my fifth book that I believe I found my signature style. *Hansel and Gretel* is the first book that I am truly proud of.

I had been working on another idea for a picture book, but I was struggling to develop any momentum so I asked Julia if she had any advice. She agreed that I needed to find a subject I really cared about – perhaps there was a fairy tale that I especially remembered from childhood? *Hansel and Gretel* immediately came to mind. I had always loved the

Above and opposite: *Hansel and Gretel*, Julia MacRae Books, 1981

single picture from the story and just see where it led. The scene I illustrated was the one in which the father and stepmother lead Hansel and Gretel into the forest to leave them there, while Hansel drops pebbles along the way to mark their route.

In many versions of the story the characters are portrayed as living in beautiful medieval cottages, dressed in classic fairytale garb (tights and jerkins, etc.), but at some point I must have decided to paint the family in modern dress – or, at least, in the fashions that were contemporary to my own fifties childhood. This decision came very naturally, because it was how I had always interpreted the story. As a child, I had applied the fairy tale to my own circumstances. Medieval hags were few and far between in 1950s northern England, and when I thought of a wicked stepmother I thought of a sour-faced, heavily made-up, middle-aged woman with a prim fifties hairdo and a leopard-skin coat. This is exactly how she appears in my illustration.

I didn't want to make my version of *Hansel and Gretel* so gloomy as to put children off, but I did want them to get a sense of the bleakness that is at the heart of the story. In too many of the versions I had seen, the illustrations applied a pretty fairytale gloss that masked the family's poverty. I wanted to make my family look every bit as poor and miserable as they are meant to be. As well as the modern dress, I think that this aspect helped to make my version distinctive.

One of the reasons that I see *Hansel and Gretel* as a breakthrough book is because I started to apply

combination of fear and delight that accompanies most fairy tales, but I got a particular frisson from reading about the terrifying adventure of *Hansel and Gretel*. The idea of being left alone in a forest by an evil stepmother and a father too pathetic to protest seemed all the more horrific in contrast to my own situation – being read the story in the comfort of my warm bed, into which I had so recently been tucked by my devoted parents.

I was aware that the story had been illustrated many times before, and this presented a new challenge for me. It was the first time I had illustrated a story that I had not written myself, and I became self-conscious as I wondered how to approach it. I wrestled with the problem for a while, but eventually decided that a good way to start would be to paint a

meaning to the hidden details. Whereas before I had considered them to be little more than doodles in the background, in *Hansel and Gretel* I employed them as subtle aids in telling the story. Not only do they reinforce the main narrative; they also offer an insight into extra narrative information that isn't expressed in the text.

Here, as the stepmother prepares to wake the children, we can see that her shadow on the wall behind her is extended by the gap in the curtains so that it appears as if she is wearing a pointed hat. As the stepmother formulates her despicable plan, the implied hat links and equates her with the witch whom the children encounter later in the story. If you look even more carefully, you can see this triangular motif is repeated several times within the picture: the shadow above the chest of drawers, the

steeple of the church in the picture on the wall, the mouse hole in the skirting board and an ambiguous object on top of the wardrobe.

Hansel and Gretel introduces another recurring feature in my books: references to famous works of art. In the first scene, the family sit around the table in a dilapidated, grimy room. On the wall behind them there is a sepia reproduction of Holman Hunt's 'Light of the World', which ironically mocks the absence of 'light' in their existence.

It was the first time I had included visual themes in a book. The two main visual themes in *Hansel and Gretel* are birds and bars, representing the opposing states of freedom and entrapment. Looking again at the first illustration in the book, we can see that the stripes on Hansel, Gretel and the father's clothing echo the bars of a cage, as do the rods on the chairs

and the striped dress of the doll on the floor. On the opposite page is a small image of the family house, dark and oppressive. The four austere trees that grow behind it combine with the literal bars on the window of the door to imprison them within its charmless walls.

The theme of birds and flight is introduced in the opening family scene. The image on the television is of an aeroplane, and there is a bird-shaped stain on the ceiling. Birds continue to appear throughout the book, either hidden in the back-

ground or as part of the main narrative. The second time the children are led into the forest, it is a white dove that Hansel claims to see on the chimney: a white bird leads them to the witch's house; birds eat the crumbs that Hansel has left to guide them home, and it is a duck that ferries the children across the lake at the end of the story.

There are a number of instances in the book where the illustration shows a scene reflected in the mirror, as if from the reader's perspective. But when we look at the image, instead of our own reflection, we see that of the characters in the story. This is my way of drawing the reader into the book. By seemingly looking into the mirror ourselves, a voyeuristic element is introduced, for we feel as if we are in the room with the characters; yet, at the same time, the absence of our own reflection makes us feel strangely excluded.

The third recurring theme in the book is that of transformation. It is evident in the implied inter-changeability of the stepmother and the witch. When the children encounter the witch – who first appears with the same illusory hat from the gap in the curtains that we saw on the stepmother's shadow earlier in the book – it is as if a transformation has taken place. The link is substantiated further when, having escaped by pushing the witch into the oven, the children return home to the news that the step-mother has also died.

The chimney of the house is transformed on each of the occasions that Hansel and Gretel are taken into the forest, firstly into a cat and secondly into a dove. And as Gretel returns from fetching water, we can see suggestions of dead birds in the roots of the tree on the left. In the moments before Hansel's imminent execution, it seems that the children's hopes of freedom – symbolized through-out the book by images of birds and flight – have also perished.

Another significant transformation occurs with the family house. When we see it again at the end of the story, the contrast with its representation on the opening page is stark. As a child, I was always

delighted by spot-the-difference puzzles, and in many of my books I have used this duplicative tech-nique. The second picture of the house is painted in brighter, paler shades of blue, green and ochre. The oppressive trees have been cut down and the bars on the windows have faded. With the stepmother dead and the children back with their loving father, this image alone conveys the sense of optimism at the end of the story.

On the opposite page is an example of a com-mon phenomenon in my books: success through the recovery from error. I originally painted the image with the children's faces visible, beaming in anticipation of their father's embrace. But just like the happy caravan holidaymakers, I couldn't make the children's smiles convincing. No matter what I tried, their expressions seemed false, their smiles contrived: they looked like irritating child actors in a silent film. I gave up. When these situations arise it always feels like an admission of failure to have to hide the area that I can't get right, and yet quite often my escape plan produces a more interesting picture. To avoid showing the children's faces, I decided to paint a view of the father from behind, with the children clinging to his legs. Only their limbs are visible from behind his body. The image is, I think, far more powerful than my original idea. A view of the faces is unnecessary. The happiness is conveyed by the gesture alone. The visible fragments

Opposite: *Hansel and Gretel*, Julia MacRae Books, 1981

of the children's bodies appear attached to their father, creating the illusion of a single figure which symbolizes the profound unity of the moment.

Hansel and Gretel remains a book for which I have a particular affection and it is also one which has a special place in Julia's affections, not least because it was the first Anthony Browne title to be published by her newly founded imprint, Julia MacRae Books. When Julia left Hamish Hamilton in 1979 to begin her own list, it was an easy decision for me to go with her; we had by then formed a close working relationship, with Julia supplying the support and encouragement so necessary to an artist's self-confidence.

Left and opposite: *Hansel and Gretel*, Julia MacRae Books, 1981

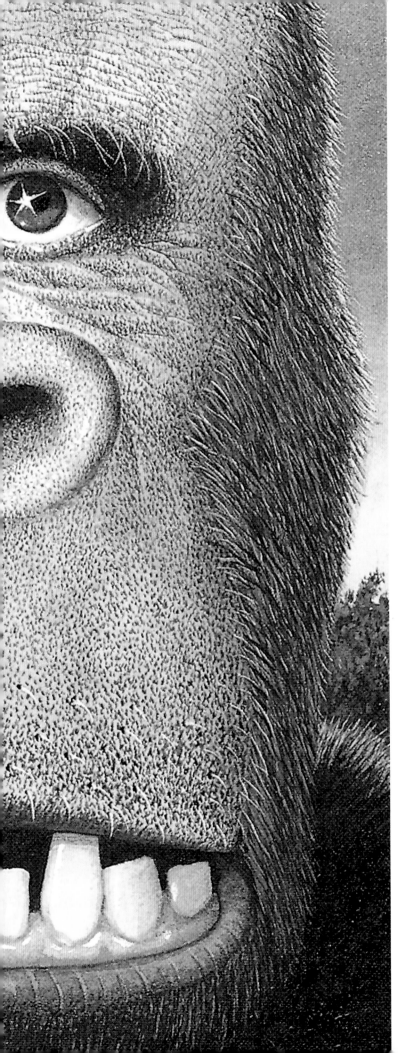

Chapter Five

Going Ape

'Why do you draw so many gorillas?' This is the most common question that I am asked by children and adults alike, and I have at least four different answers.

Firstly, they are fascinating creatures to look at. I have spent hours watching gorillas in zoos (I have yet to see them in the wild, but I would love to), and I could happily study their faces all day. Old people's faces are far more interesting to draw than young people's because of the patterns and contours of the aged skin; gorilla faces are more appealing still. The wrinkles and lumps and bumps and swellings and hair and muscle are irresistible to the pencil. I could never tire of drawing them.

Secondly, they are so much like people. Looking into a gorilla's eyes is almost exactly like looking into a person's eyes, and if I look for long enough it seems as though there is another human being inside the gorilla, looking back at me. It is an eerie yet exhilarating experience. They are so much like us.

Thirdly, they remind me of my father. He was a big, strong, quite fierce-looking man, with an aggressive streak which he saved for the rugby field, the boxing ring and the war zone. This made him a hero to Michael and me: we wanted to do all the same things. But while he encouraged us to be physical, there was another side of him that was extremely gentle. Dad was just as happy drawing with us, telling us stories or writing us poems as he was teaching us how to tackle. I think of Dad when I look at gorillas. Gorillas are immensely powerful creatures and can be terrifyingly aggressive when they want to be, but they also have a gentle side which they express by grooming each other, showing affection and caring for their families.

Another answer was given for me. I was talking to some children in a bookshop many years ago, and a little lad asked me the question about gorillas. Somebody usually does. But this time, instead of reciting one of my rehearsed answers, I decided to turn the question back on him: 'Why do *you* think I draw so many gorillas?'

He thought about it for a while and then said that gorillas are a bit like my pictures. When you first look at my pictures they seem normal, but if you look closer you realize that they're not quite. He used *Piggybook* as an example. The picture of the family in the living room doesn't seem unusual at first, but if you look again you notice that the door handle has changed into a pig's face and the flower in the man's buttonhole is in the shape of a pig. He said that the same is true of gorillas. They appear to be 'normal' (in his sense of the word, i.e. like people), but they're not quite. I thought it was a brilliant answer and I am grateful to that little boy to this day. He was right. Gorillas represent a strange departure from humanity, which ties in well with the surreal, alternative version of reality that I present in my books.

The first book that featured a gorilla prominently was actually called *Gorilla*. It was published in 1983 and it is still my favourite book of those I have made. While working on *Gorilla* I felt that it was the first time I had really understood how to make a picture book, in the sense that the words and pictures

Chapter opener: *Gorilla*, Julia MacRae Books, 1983

Right: *Gorilla*, Julia MacRae Books, 1983

worked both together *and* apart.

Hannah loves gorillas. She reads books about gorillas, she watches gorillas on the television, she draws pictures of gorillas; but she has never seen a real gorilla. Her father is very cold and aloof, and never 'has the time' to take her to the zoo. Whenever she tries to talk to him about anything he is either too busy or too tired. They never do anything together.

The night before her birthday, Hannah is very excited because her father has agreed to get her a gorilla, but she wakes up in the middle of the night to find a disappointingly small parcel at the foot of her bed. She opens it and finds that the promised gorilla is only a toy. Hannah discards it in the corner of her room and goes back to sleep. In the night, however, 'something amazing happens'. The toy becomes a real gorilla. The gorilla puts on her father's hat and coat and takes Hannah on a fantastic night-time adventure. They do everything she has always wanted to do with her father. They go to the zoo to see the primates; they go to the cinema; they have a delicious meal together and they end the night by dancing on the lawn. Hannah is desperately happy.

She wakes up the next morning and finds that the gorilla is a toy once more. She goes downstairs to see her father, who, for the first time, shows warmth and affection. He offers to take her to the zoo. The final image is of the two of them walking to the zoo together, the toy gorilla in Hannah's hand.

The inspiration for the story has three sources.

When I was a small boy of about six, I asked my parents if they would get me a trumpet for my birthday. I had been listening to the records of Eddie Calvert, especially the tune, 'Mein Papa'. I wanted to be just like him. If I had my very own shiny trumpet I too could make that wonderful sound. I awoke very early on the morning of my birthday and sure enough there was a trumpet-sized parcel at the foot of my bed. I opened it up and inside was a cardboard box with a cellophane front, containing the shiniest trumpet I had ever seen. But something wasn't right. It was *too* shiny somehow, and when I picked it up it was far lighter than I had expected. I didn't know anything about trumpets – I had never even held one – but I was suspicious all the same. I took it out of its cellophane packaging (packaging for a trumpet? Where was the smart black case?) and blew it. A pathetic, flat, plastic sound came out. It was awful.

I didn't want my parents to see my disappointment, so I made a point of playing the toy trumpet constantly for the next few days. It was only capable of four very flat notes, so it didn't take me long to learn all the tunes in the accompanying book. To this day (if I choose to) I can close my eyes and hear my unique rendition of 'Come to the Cookhouse Door'.

After a short time, I lost interest in the trumpet. I discarded it in the corner of my bedroom, but it never became real and I never showed any interest in learning a musical instrument again.

Gorilla was also influenced by the film *King Kong*.

I first saw it when I was at art college, and I remember being fascinated by the vulnerability of Fay Wray's character, literally in the hands of the giant ape. It was a fantastic contrast. Something about the unlikely affection that develops between them always appealed to me, and it is unsurprising that a similar relationship eventually surfaced in my work.

The third inspiration for the book was Trajan. Trajan was a little boy who lived in the same village as me. He rarely saw his father, who lived in New Zealand, and I think he adopted me as a substitute for him. Trajan knew that I worked at home, and he would come to the house very early each morning – often dressed in his Superman outfit – to work alongside me. He was very creative, and would spend all day drawing or making things. While I was working on *Gorilla* he made a gorilla's head out of wire and papier-mâché. It was brilliant. Like Hannah in the story, Trajan desperately needed the attention of a father figure.

There are several illustrations in *Gorilla* that demonstrate my emergent understanding of picture books. As with the two images of the family house in *Hansel and Gretel*, the two meal scenes in *Gorilla* are the result of my childhood preoccupation with spot-the-difference puzzles. In some ways the images are very similar. Compositionally, they both show the back of Hannah's head as she eats her meal, with the foreshortened table stretching towards a male character sitting opposite her. But certain visual clues ensure that the pictures tell very different stories. In the first illustration, Hannah is

Above: *Gorilla*, Julia MacRae Books, 1983

positioned at the very bottom of the frame, and the angle of the scene makes it appear as though we are looking through Hannah's eyes up towards her father at the top of the image. I have exaggerated the perspective of the table so that the distance between them seems greater. Hannah's father doesn't talk to her; he doesn't listen to her; he just reads his paper, which he holds up like a wall between them, deflecting her attempts to establish intimacy.

We can't actually see any food on the table. The only evidence that a meal is taking place is the cereal box. Everything in the kitchen is impeccably clean and tidy, and the neatness of the room is emphasized by the proliferation of geometric shapes and designs.

Apart from Hannah, who is painted in a vibrant, optimistic red, the colour scheme is almost entirely blue. Blue, of course, carries the connotations of sadness, and there is little joy in the picture. But the colours also give the scene a cold, icy quality – an effect which is enhanced by the main feature of the room: a giant fridge. This huge monument of coldness is like an altar which frames Hannah's unapproachable father.

In the second meal scene, I have flattened the perspective so that Hannah is nearer to the gorilla and nearer to the viewer. It is a closer shot, which makes the reader feel more included in the scene. The two characters appear physically closer than they did in the first illustration, and their proximity is far more conducive to interaction. There is a copious amount of food on the table; the shapes of the various objects and patterns are unpredictable

Opposite and right: *Gorilla*, Julia MacRae Books, 1983

and organic; and the bright colours – reds, yellows, oranges and browns – give the picture a warm glow.

I used the spot-the-difference concept again with the picture of Hannah and the gorilla walking hand-in-hand to the restaurant and the final picture of her walking to the zoo with her father. There are very few differences this time. The two images are intended to show the link between the gorilla and Hannah's father. This link is substantiated by the fact that the gorilla wears her father's hat and coat throughout their adventure, and the penultimate illustration shows the father with a banana sticking out of his back pocket. I wanted children to identify the connection for themselves, but I didn't want to insult their intelligence by making it too obvious. The clues are subtle, but the amount of letters I have received from children who have noticed the link leads me to believe that I got the balance just right.

In most picture books there are a number of illustrations that have a purely transitional function. Their role is simply to link one episode of the story to the next. I have talked to several illustrators about these pictures and most agree that they represent the least interesting part of illustrating a children's book. The picture of Hannah walking upstairs to bed on the night before her birthday is one such illustration. In order to make the process more interesting I found myself developing strategies designed to motivate me as I painted the picture. Hannah's mind is fixed on gorillas at this point, and I have tried to show this with visual clues. There is a gorilla version of the 'Mona Lisa' on the wall behind her, and the knob on the end of the banister looks like a gorilla's head. Trying to imagine how I could illustrate Hannah's psychological landscape made the experience far more entertaining, and I have tried to adopt a similar approach to transitional illustrations ever since.

While I was working on *Gorilla*, my publisher suggested that I appear on a television programme for schools to talk about picture books for older children. The director of the film latched onto the gorilla theme. He decided to have me and other characters in the film wear gorilla masks for part of it, and he wanted the highlight of the programme to be me in the gorilla cage at the zoo, meeting my first gorilla. The television company contacted Howletts Zoo, near where I lived in Kent. The zoo agreed to let me be filmed in the cage, but they advised that I spend some time getting to know the gorillas in the weeks before the filming.

I went to Howletts twice in consecutive weeks, and spent an hour each time in the cage with two female gorillas and a baby gorilla. This was how it was to be in the film. I thought it would be more dramatic if I was shown meeting a huge male gorilla, but the first time I went into the cage I was glad of the zoo's precautions. One of the females approached me as soon as I entered. I had been told by the keeper to kneel down to her level and not to look directly into her eyes so that I would not be interpreted as a threat. But before I could do so, the gorilla grabbed hold of my leg and propelled me into the middle of the cage. Her strength was awe-inspiring. I was totally helpless. All those years playing rugby against big strong men did nothing to prepare me for such unbelievable power. I was like a rag doll. Apparently she did it

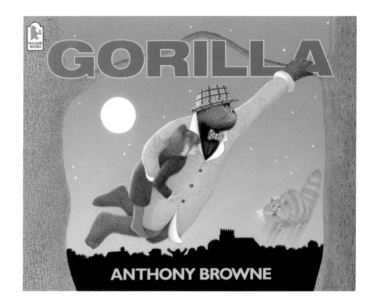

because I was a stranger and yet to prove that I was no threat. It was only a small demonstration to show me who was boss, but it certainly worked.

After the dramatic introduction, the gorillas spent the rest of the session investigating me. I knelt down with the keeper, and the gorillas took it in turns to sniff me, climb on my back and inspect my hair. Once they got used to me they became more playful, and we settled into a kind of play-boxing encounter during which I was careful to look down at all times. They were quite gentle and gave no impression that they wanted to hurt me, but looking back at the experience I realize how terrifying it was. It was like being in a cage with two mad men with superhuman strength. They moved unpredictably, they made strange, unreadable noises and I never knew what they were going to do next. The thought that they could destroy me in an instant made the encounter incredibly frightening.

Part of me didn't want to spend another minute with the gorillas, but the thrill was intoxicating, and another part of me longed to repeat the experience. I also felt obligated. The project was a big deal for me. The television crew were travelling from London to Kent, staying the night at a hotel and filming me walking on the streets of Canterbury as if I was a celebrity, even though I wasn't at all well known. I was very flattered and didn't feel I was in a position to deny the director his big idea. I felt I *had* to go back in the cage.

The second rehearsal did little to assuage my nerves. Again I was investigated by the gorillas; again we played; again I was both excited and terrified. But just before I left the cage, one of the gorillas looked me straight in the eye – demanding that I look back – and fixed her teeth around my arm, never once relaxing her potent stare. I was wearing a thick pullover and a tough jacket, so it didn't break the skin, but it *did* hurt, and I could feel the immense power of her teeth and jaws. It was another warning: *just remember what I can do to you if you get out of line, mate.* I had spent two hours with the gorillas in preparation for the filming, but I wasn't yet their friend.

The day of the filming arrived. The cameramen were not to enter the cage themselves, so they set up their equipment just outside. Once everything was prepared I was told to go ahead and enter the cage. Part of me felt as if I was being told to walk the plank.

In order to prevent the gorillas from escaping,

there was a tight security arrangement, and to get to the animals one had to pass through three sets of doors. As I walked through the doors I could see that the gorillas were behaving oddly. They were shaking the bars of the cage and making awful shrieking noises – running crazily from one end of the enclosure to the other, before returning to the bars and pounding them with their fists. Needless to say, it was all a little disconcerting. As I progressed, I became aware that something was going on in the far corner of the cage. The owner of Howletts Zoo, John Aspinall, was tossing what looked like roses into the enclosure. I didn't think much about it at the time because I was too busy worrying about the gorillas' behaviour. As soon as I walked through the third door one of the gorillas approached me, and I bent down to pat her on the back like a dog, trying to convey my friendliness at this time of unrest. The gorilla was having none of it. Without warning she sank her teeth into my calf, producing the most excruciating pain I have ever known. The programme was for schoolchildren, and I was wearing a clip-on microphone so that I could describe to my young viewers how it felt to encounter a gorilla for the first time. But I wasn't expecting to be bitten by a gorilla, and the first words that I uttered had to be bleeped out on the final edit!

The gorilla clung on for a while, but with a combination of my fist and the keeper's foot she

Opposite: *Gorilla*, Julia MacRae Books, 1983
Overleaf: *Willy the Wimp*, Julia MacRae Books, 1984

eventually ran off, leaving me in a heap on the ground – and an embarrassing dilemma. I knew I was badly hurt. The pain was terrible, and I could see through the hole in my jeans, which were rapidly turning purple, that the wound was horrific. But I was embarrassed to tell the television people that I needed to go to hospital immediately. It seemed as though they had travelled down from London just to help my career, and I was loath to call the filming off because of something as trivial as a gorilla bite! As I was kneeling down, nobody could see my leg, so I was able to pretend that everything was all right for a while. When the keeper asked if I was OK, I said something stupid like, 'Yes, fine . . . I may never dance again!' (Actually, I could never dance in the first place!)

I was wary that the gorilla might return, and my nerves were not helped by the fact that the keeper, who knew the gorillas very well, also seemed anxious. He leaned in to me and dropped a bombshell. The reason the gorilla had bitten me was because of the roses that Aspinall had thrown into the cage. Rose petals are an exquisite delicacy to gorillas, given to them only every now and then as a special treat. The gorilla had bitten me as a warning not to go near the petals. But it was only a warning. Had she wanted to, she could have taken my leg clean off. The keeper also said that Aspinall knew exactly what he was doing.

I knelt there, bleeding into my jeans, for twenty minutes. Every time a gorilla came near, the keeper shooed it off. I had raised the television crew's

expectations by telling them about all the playing and jostling and grooming that I had done with the gorillas in rehearsals, but this made for very uneventful viewing. Two men cowering in the corner of a cage was nothing like the magical TV moment the director had envisioned. Eventually the crew got wind that something was badly wrong, and when they saw the colour of my jeans they took me to hospital immediately.

I found out later that there had been a dispute between Aspinall and the television company about how much money they were able to pay him. They were only a small company, and they were obviously unable to pay as much as the BBC who had filmed at Howletts three weeks before. Aspinall would not accept this, and it seemed that he made his point by punishing me: by releasing his rather unusual 'hounds', so to speak.

The experience hasn't put me off gorillas at all, but I certainly have no desire to share a cage with them ever again.

Gorilla was the first of my books to feature an ape, and it launched my reputation as the gorilla man. Since then I have produced a lot of books with simian characters, and my name has become synonymous with gorillas and chimpanzees. This is largely due to my most prolific and successful character, Willy. I don't remember why I chose to make Willy a chimpanzee, but his character origins are more palpable. The way in which Willy copes with life is child-like. I am often asked if the character is based on me. I suppose he is to an

extent, but I believe that I fall into a large group of people who had similar experiences as children. As the younger sibling, I grew up in the constant shadow of my older brother, and much of my childhood seemed like a hopeless competition. He would always beat me at everything. I often felt small and pathetic, and it sometimes seemed as if I was a different species to Michael and his friends. Willy is a chimpanzee, living in a world of gorillas. The gorillas are bigger, stronger, more powerful and more important than he is. Throughout our lives, we often find ourselves in situations where we feel inferior to the majority of people around us, but I think the sensation is particularly familiar to children. Children live in a world that is dominated by adults. In this world they are smaller, weaker, more ignorant, less influential, and they spend their lives being bossed about by older brothers and sisters, parents and teachers. Life can be over-whelmingly intimidating and Willy's situation,

though metaphorical, is poignantly resonant among children. He is easily my most popular character, and I have received hundreds of letters from young readers who identify with him.

Willy the Wimp is about Willy – a gentle soul who 'wouldn't hurt a fly'. He worries about treading on tiny insects as he walks and apologizes to others when **they** knock into him. Willy endures constant bullying by the gorillas: Willy the Wimp, they call him.

One day Willy sees an advertisement in a comic for a course: 'Don't be a wimp!' He applies for the course, and after a vigorous programme of exercises and weightlifting, he builds himself up until he is big enough to take on the gorillas. He sees the gorillas attacking Millie, the girl of his fancy, and they flee at the sight of the new-look chimpanzee. Millie tells Willy that he is her hero, and he appears inflated with pride as he walks away. The final sequence, however, shows him colliding with a lamppost and immediately apologizing. He hasn't really changed.

One of the main influences for *Willy the Wimp* was the Bonzo Dog Doo Dah Band. They were a brilliant comedy band, led by Viv Stanshall, which used to play regularly at the art college. Not only did they share my interests in both surrealism and gorillas, but their sense of humour was totally compatible with mine. The song, 'Mr Apollo', is about a bodybuilding visionary. In the form of an advertisement for a weightlifting course, it features Viv Stanshall as the title character, describing his

DONT BE A *WIMP!*

I <u>was</u> a scrawny, skinny-chested
pathetic weakling. NOW..........
I can order people about..........
kick sand in THEIR faces...
talk VERY LOUDLY.....
lift heavy things......
get R·E·S·P·E·C·T.
Do YOU want..........
Bulging arm muscles..
Tireless legs..........
A deep chest............
A large wardrobe............
A magnetic personality?
POST THIS *NOW!*

Willy completes the course, which includes jogging, aerobics, boxing and, of course, body-building. When I painted the illustration of Willy with his fellow bodybuilders, I wanted to get their anatomies and poses just right, so I went into my local newsagent to buy a bodybuilding magazine. The only one they had was on the top shelf along with the pornography. It was wrapped in the same opaque polythene as its neighbours, but I could see that the cover featured an enormous couple in tiny swimming costumes. Everything about it was dubious. Not only was I embarrassed about buying the magazine but I was also shocked at its price:

Opposite, above and right: *Willy the Wimp*, Julia MacRae Books, 1984

path to physical superiority in a ridiculous voice, before listing the various benefits of his course.

When I came to write the plot for *Willy the Wimp*, I decided that Willy would attempt to match the gorillas by building up his body. Send-away bodybuilding courses are less common nowadays, but I remember seeing similar advertisements for Charles Atlas courses in comics when I was a boy. But Charles Atlas has nothing to do with the pro-gramme that Willy applies for. I don't state it overtly, but the implication is that the course is run by Stanshall's inimitable Mr Apollo. The advertisement even goes as far as paraphrasing a line from the song about kicking the sand back in their faces.

presumably the guiltiest of pleasures come at a cost. It didn't help that I was nine-and-a-half stone, so my motive was clearly something other than the pursuit of professional advice.

I grabbed the magazine and dashed to the counter. It seemed as if fifteen people or so instantly formed a queue behind me, anticipating my humiliation. *Roll up, roll up!* I wanted the experience to be over as quickly as possible, so I made sure I had exactly the right amount of money in my hand. I put the magazine on the counter. The lady at the till gasped and then bawled at me in astonishment, 'Do you know how much this costs, love?'

I smiled through the sweat and replied, 'Yes, I know . . . But this is the one they said they wanted!'

I thought afterwards that this was exactly what Willy would have said under the circumstances. There is undeniably a little of me in him.

Willy the Wimp was something of a breakthrough for me in terms of design. Previously I had just painted the illustrations in boxes, and worked the text around them. Sometimes I had a small box containing a small illustration on the left-hand page with a lot of text underneath, and a much larger box on the right, but apart from that there was little variation. I was concerned that the story of *Willy the Wimp* was quite serious, so I wanted the illustrations to compensate by being as light and fresh and lively as possible. I did this by varying the design of the pictures all the way through the book. The first page shows Willy as a lone figure against a large white background, and the subsequent pages vary considerably. Some of the images are boxed as before; some spreads have the text on one side and a large illustration that bleeds to the very edges of the opposite page; one of the pictures is painted

Left and opposite: *Willy the Wimp,*
Julia MacRae Books, 1984

with 'torn edges' to appear as if it has been ripped out of a comic; some of the pictures have circular frames and there are occasional vignettes amid the text; and there is a kind of animation sequence as Willy lifts the barbell, with four increasingly large images of him getting bigger over time. The accompanying text for this sequence also increases in size. When Willy walks away from the scene of his triumph at the end, there is another sequence of pictures that is intended to suggest animation, painted in four successive boxes like frames in a film.

The final picture of Willy apologizing to the lamppost is deliberately painted with no visual context – we can't see the top of the lamppost or any surrounding objects – so it is unclear whether or not Willy has shrunk back to his original size. I intended the ending to be ambiguous, but some people misinterpreted it completely. Those who

thought that Willy had shrunk couldn't understand why. I reminded them that the point of the story is that any physical transformation Willy may or may not undergo is irrelevant. The ending is intended to show that, despite the apparent augmentation of his body, his personality remains the same. It is not important whether or not his body shrinks in the final picture: the only thing that we can be sure *does* shrink is his ego.

Willy went on to become my most reliable and most recognizable ape, but the *Willy* series is part of a plethora of books that feature gorillas and chimpanzees.

In 1994 I decided to make a book about the most famous gorilla of all. I had produced a lot of picture books by this stage and fancied the challenge of doing something a little more epic. I wanted to produce a longer work that was something between

Above and opposite: *King Kong*, Julia MacRae Books, 1994

a picture book and a novel, and *King Kong* seemed an obvious choice. I had always loved the film and had toyed with the idea of converting it into a book, but previously deemed it too long and daunting a project. Now I felt I was ready.

I first saw the film at art college, and whether or not it was deliberately included in the series, it was screened during a season of surrealist films. This association stayed with me, and although I don't necessarily think of it as surrealist, I certainly view *King Kong* as a serious film as opposed to the commercial moneymaking movie that it was reputedly meant to be.

The story of the film is in fact very personal. The obsessive determination of the fictional director, Karl Denham, to get his movie made is not dissimilar to the endeavours of *King Kong's* real life director, Merian C. Cooper. *King Kong* is a film about making a film, with money as the motive.

Everything about the story appealed to me. The contrast between the giant gorilla and the tiny, beautiful woman is fascinating on many levels, and I love the development of the plot, which forces the viewer to change his or her perceptions throughout its course. When we first encounter Kong, we assume that he is brutal, cruel and terrifying, but as the story develops we realize that he is in fact sensitive and humane. His violence is only a response to his exploitation. The real monsters in the story are his human captors.

I decided to adapt the film into a very long picture book. When children get to a certain age they are encouraged by their parents to switch from picture books to pictureless books, and this can be a difficult transition for some. My concern is that children who struggle to make the sudden 'upgrade' can be put off reading altogether. *King Kong* was an attempt to bridge the gap.

I tried to make the reading experience resemble that of watching a movie, with a picture on every page, each image representing a frame in the film. My intention was to maintain much of the style of the original movie, while portraying the gorilla more sympathetically than Cooper did.

I wanted to base the text on a literary version of the film which had been released at the same time. The use of this text, and indeed of any visual image of King Kong, required long and complex negotiations with the American owners of copyrights in the material, but Julia, who was also a *King Kong* fan, persevered, and eventually we were given permission both to go ahead with the book and to use the text I wanted because its dialogue and descriptions were so characteristic of 1930s New York.

Deciding on a model for the female lead, Anne Darrow, was

difficult. Most of my characters were based on the actors in the original film, but as appropriate as Fay Wray was for the role at the time, I didn't feel that her face transcended society's fickle conceptions of beauty over time. I often use people I know as models for my illustrations – my children's joints have no doubt become stiff from the accumulated hours of dutiful posing – but although I know some good-looking people, I couldn't think of anybody with the kind of Hollywood beauty that was required for the part. Like Denham in the movie, I took to scouring the streets, looking for just the right woman. Alas, I wasn't to find her among the Kent shoppers, and in the end I decided to model Anne Darrow on the ultimate cinema beauty: Marilyn Monroe. The decision seemed to make sense because not only is Monroe timelessly beautiful but her exploitation by Hollywood echoes that of Kong himself. I tried to suggest this by painting Darrow's hair dark at the beginning of the book (like Monroe in her pre-stardom identity as Norma Jean King), but as soon as she joins the film crew she transforms into the blonde bombshell that we all recognize. The symbolic bleaching that she undergoes for the voyage to Skull Island coincides with the start of the moral descent.

I have often said that making a picture book is like planning a film. The early stages involve drawing up a storyboard which looks like a series of frames, and when I think of an idea it frequently comes to me in the form of an animated scene. Tackling *King Kong* was essentially the reverse of this process. The film was already in place and my task was to turn it into a picture book. I struggled with this unfamiliar approach, and it was an exhausting book to produce, both physically and mentally. It was a real effort to maintain the same quality as I painted picture after picture after picture. I started painting quite realistically, with the same care and attention to detail that I had always employed, but, as when I ran the mile at school, I was in danger of putting too much effort into the early stages without having the endurance to sustain the same standard until the end. *King Kong* required far more pictures than any other book I have made – almost as many as a graphic novel. I hadn't prepared myself for the size of the undertaking, and there were times when I lost enthusiasm for the whole project. But I stuck with it and finally managed to complete what is my most difficult book to date.

One of the problems I faced with converting the film into a picture book was how to handle the slow opening. Kong doesn't appear at all for the first quarter of the movie, but although the action is minimal, the filmmakers had several cinematic techniques at their disposal to help reduce the

audience's impatience. It isn't as easy with a picture book. My solution was to draw upon my reliable technique of painting hidden clues and references in an attempt to heighten the anticipation of Kong's introduction. For the uneventful café scene in which Denham tries to persuade Anne Darrow to appear in his picture (without mentioning her fifty-foot screen partner) I tried to show what was going on

in his mind by working a gorilla's face into the burger on the left-hand illustration. On the opposite page, a poster on the wall advertises GARGANTUA THE GREAT – THE LARGEST GORILLA EVER EXHIBITED. There is also a suggestion of a gorilla's hand in the glove that protrudes from the coat hanging up beside it.

On the next page, as Anne wakes up on the boat, we can see a gorilla's face in the pattern of the wood grain on the wall. Turn over again, and the badge on the First Mate's cap looks strangely like a gorilla, as does Anne's shadow as she screams for Denham's sinisterly orchestrated rehearsal.

Kong epitomizes everything that I love about gorillas. He is strong, powerful and destructive, but he has a loving heart that softens the menace.

Opposite and right:
King Kong, Julia MacRae Books, 1994

The book is dedicated to my father, who really was the original Kong for me. Painting the images of Kong falling from the Empire State was an emotional experience, because it reminded me of Dad collapsing and dying in front of me. I am pleased that I was able to pay tribute to my great father in a book about my favourite gorilla.

King Kong is the most powerful and heroic of all the apes I have portrayed, but he carries a link to the most feeble and apologetic: Willy. Willy is alienated because he is a chimpanzee living among gorillas. Kong is alienated because *he* is the gorilla, surrounded by smaller, weaker human beings. Both are outsiders.

Above, opposite and overleaf:
Willy and Hugh, Julia MacRae Books, 1991

I brought the two types together in a book that I made not long after *King Kong*, called *Willy and Hugh*. At the beginning of the book, Willy is lonely, and he envies the gorillas he sees having fun with their friends. Then one day he literally bumps into Hugh Jape.

Hugh is a gorilla like all the others, but after their collision it is Hugh who apologizes first to Willy! Willy and Hugh realize that they have a lot in common and they become friends. Hugh is Willy's King Kong. He is big and strong and imposing when he wants to be – he shows this by defending Willy from Buster Nose when he comes looking for the 'little wimp' – but he is also kind, sensitive and occasionally vulnerable.

Willy's triumphant moment is when he helps Hugh by carefully removing a spider which is the

source of his friend's terror. Although Willy and Hugh appear very different, they are in fact very similar, and like all good friends they are happy to help each other out in times of weakness. Their fondness for each other is confirmed on the very last page, which shows them meeting the day after the events of the story.

Touchingly, they have each tried to look like the other, with Willy switching from his usual green corduroy trousers to a pair of jeans, and Hugh sporting a sleeveless pullover that is similar to Willy's trademark top.

There is no one consistent reason why I use gorillas and chimpanzees for my characters: it always depends on the individual book.

What I really like about apes as a subject is their

universality. The apes that I write about are people in all but appearance. They behave like people, they talk like people and they dress like people; yet to look at them, they are clearly animals, disguised as people. I think we should be reminded of the fact that people are essentially apes too: our genetic makeup is almost identical, our desires and instincts are the same, and we don't even look all that different. The boundaries between humans and animals are nowhere near as distinct as we like to believe, and the humanization of apes in my books is partly my attempt to blur the divide. But it also blurs other divides. The universality of the simian characters ensures that all children can identify with them – not just those who are of the same age, era or ethnicity. Willy is a chimpanzee and therefore doesn't look like any child, but in another sense he looks like every child, and it delights me when I receive confirmation of his universal appeal. One of the greatest letters I have ever received was from a child who wanted to know about Willy. It said,

Dear Anthony Browne,

Is Willy a real person, or did you make him up?

These few words seem to answer the ape question in as succinct and brilliant a way as possible. I love the fact that the child saw Willy as a person, and was able to look beyond Willy's appearance to see the young child (probably him or herself) inside. My other favourite letter was from a little boy called Bret in Australia. It wasn't addressed to me but to Willy, and it contained one of the greatest pieces of advice that he or anyone has ever received. It said,

Dear Willy,

You don't have to be big and strong.
Just watch where you're going.

Chapter Six
Family Values

Willy stands out from my other characters because he is usually depicted on his own. Although we see him in company occasionally, it is noticeable that he is never shown with his family, for many of my stories are set within a family environment.

Families have always been an important part of my life. As a child, I was part of a very close family, and when I grew up I started a new family which was equally loving. Having spent most of my life in a family environment, and having known and observed many other families, I believe I have learned a lot about them, and as most children live under a strong influence exerted by their parents and siblings, it has always been a natural subject for my books.

I have portrayed many families over the years and they are all different. Although I write extensively about the love and tenderness within families, I also like to address the difficulties of family life, and few of the families that I write about are without their problems. A lot of people have suggested that the majority of these problems stem from the fathers. It is a popular belief that I portray fathers in a negative light. I have become quite defensive in the past when faced with these claims, but I can see what has given the critics this impression. The fathers in my books display a vast array of character flaws: the father in *Hansel and Gretel* is weak and hen-pecked; the father in *Gorilla* is distant and cold; the father in *Piggybook* is lazy; Mr Young in *The Big Baby* is vain, and 'Dad' in *Zoo* is simply a buffoon.

I think that one of the reasons I give fathers a bit of a hard time is related to my own father. Although I remember him with nothing but love and admiration, perhaps on a subconscious level I have harboured a little anger towards him (albeit irrational) because he left at such a crucial time in my life.

The other reason is self-consciousness. Some people are inclined to think that certain characters represent the author's alter ego. After I had children, I naturally shied away from portraying loving, competent fathers, because I was worried that people might think it was how I assessed myself.

But I think that all the fathers in my books should attract some sympathy. Being a parent is a difficult responsibility, and many of the men that I seem to ridicule are simply miscast in the role.

Piggybook is the book that ignited the issue. It is about Mr and Mrs Piggott and their two sons, Simon and Patrick.

The responsibility for maintaining the house and family is entirely dumped upon the mother, who is habitually bullied into submission by the constant demands of her lazy husband and sons. While she does everything to make them comfortable, they slouch around and watch television, completely oblivious to her tireless exertions. But one day the mother flips. The males arrive home to find that she has gone, leaving nothing but a note on the mantelpiece bearing the simple statement, 'You are pigs'. The illustration shows the father's hand, which has turned into a pig's trotter, holding the note. Whether or not Mrs Piggott intended her statement to be metaphorical, her family have literally become the pigs that they always resembled.

The males are helpless in Mum's absence. After

Chapter opener: Michael and me, c.1959

Above: *Piggybook*, Julia MacRae Books, 1986

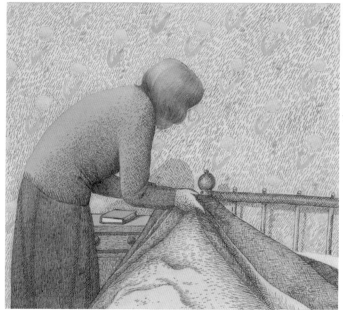

days of disastrous attempts to cook for themselves and continual neglect of the washing up, the house becomes a pigsty. Very soon they realize how lost they are without Mrs Piggott and are desperate for her to return.

The pigs run out of food and are forced to root around for edible morsels amid the filth. At the pinnacle of their depravity, the mother enters the house. They beg her to come back. She agrees to stay, but she has several conditions which are illustrated over the next few pages. Mr Piggott is shown washing the dishes and doing the ironing while Simon and Patrick make the beds. They all help with the cooking, and the final page shows Mrs Piggott fixing the car.

Piggybook is probably the most moral book I have ever made. The family dynamic in the story is probably quite common, but it was loosely based on one particular family that I knew. Interestingly, after the book was published and I gave a copy to the family in question, they showed no signs of recognizing themselves.

Although it isn't a particularly large book, *Piggybook* was to be one of the longest projects I had ever undertaken. After discussion about the initial idea, I was given a contract and advance by my publisher, so went ahead, completing a dummy and several illustrations. I could tell from Julia's unusually lukewarm response to this that something about the work was troubling her, and I was not altogether happy myself. The book at this stage had a negative quality, but I liked the idea and was disappointed and not a little irritated by the reaction to it. I could not put my finger on just why it didn't work, so I put it away for a while and concentrated on something else. The original dummy for *Piggybook* and a couple of pieces of finished artwork were put away in a drawer and there they stayed for some considerable time until, much later, I opened the drawer and looked at them again. This time I saw instantly what was wrong with it. The break from the book proved to be exactly what I had needed, for since removing it from the forefront of my mind, I had subconsciously solved the problem. I had drawn the pigs too realistically. Instead of the light-hearted, colourful book that I had intended to produce, the realistic pigs' heads atop the human bodies gave the pictures a horrific quality. The grotesque mythological monsters I had created were not only frightening to look at but they also gave the book an unwanted moral heaviness.

There was also very little humour in it. The hidden references to pigs that are everywhere in the final publication were absent from the first attempt: there were no jokes.

When I returned to the book I transformed everything. The realistic pigs became cartoon-like, child-friendly creatures – more like the animals I used to depict on greetings cards – and I saturated the book with humour. The colours (of which pink is the prevailing shade) are much brighter and optimistic, which helped to remove the weightiness

Opposite and below:
Piggybook, Julia MacRae Books, 1986

Top: The original 'grotesque mythological monsters', 1984
Left and opposite: *Piggybook*, Julia MacRae Books, 1986

of the aborted version. Now, when the family turned into pigs, it felt less like a biblical punishment and more like a mildly didactic joke.

I painted pig motifs liberally throughout the early part of the book. They are everywhere from the illustrations on the cereal packets to the flower in Mr Piggott's buttonhole – partly as a joke, and partly as a means of foreshadowing the events later in the story.

The ending is ambiguous. I always wanted the mother to stay, but it is far more interesting to allow for a dash of uncertainty.

The final page shows Mrs Piggott fixing the car, and although she is smiling, the number plate of the car reads SGIP321 (123 PIGS backwards), which dampens the optimism ever so slightly. It could just be a little joke, but it could also be an indication that not everything is as fine as it seems.

Although the family have made some important changes, we cannot help but wonder how long it will be before the males revert to their old ways. I am pleased with my decision to have the ending this way, but it did create a few problems. When I saw the German edition of *Piggybook*, I thought that the final page seemed to have far too many words. I didn't speak any German, but still I doubted that a translation of the sentence 'She fixed the car' required nearly four lines of text. When I showed it to a German friend of mine, she offered this rough translation: '"And I will check that there's enough oil in the motor, I swear!" she said, and she went outside. Mr Piggott, Simon and Patrick heard the car start.'

My German editor had decided to turn the ending upside down by implying that Mrs Piggott leaves her family for ever. I couldn't believe it: with one blow of his pen he had transformed my simple story about male indolence into an overblown feminist text. It was, admittedly, an interesting take on the ending, but his job wasn't to adapt, it was to translate.

Piggybook may be the most moral of my works, but I have frequently divided opinions throughout my career. The family which appears in the books *Zoo* and *The Shape Game* has also attracted controversy.

Zoo was a book that I had been quietly developing for a long time. I have always found zoos fascinating: they delight and appal me in equal measure. I love to look at the animals, and I realize that zoos help to protect certain endangered species, but I am uncomfortable with the notion of removing animals from their natural environment, imprisoning them, and exhibiting them to the public.

I decided to express these feelings in a book about a family day out at the zoo. I wanted to tell the story from the point of view of a young boy because it would allow for a healthy amount of childish humour which would counterbalance the more serious message about the nature of zoos. As I was to tell the story with a young boy's voice, it made perfect sense to take advantage of a very useful resource that I had at the time: a nine-year-old son, Joe. I took Joe to the zoo and we both noted our observations about the animals' behaviour and the comments of the spectators. With these observations as a starting point, Joe then wrote an extended short story. It was very funny. Much of

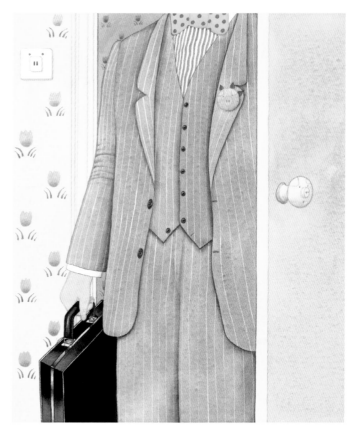

the humour was focused around the father of the family, who was Joe's prize creation. Part Homer Simpson and part camp commandant, Dad is a large, irritable man who blunders his way through fatherhood with a mixture of mistimed rebukes and terrible jokes. It was a great story, told in just the right style, and I decided to base my version on Joe's draft.

The plot is simple. Told from the point of view of the elder of two brothers, it describes a trip to the zoo. Dad is crotchety from the start, but he punctuates his tantrums with sub-Christmas-cracker jokes, which he alone finds hilarious.

The family look at a variety of animals but, apart from Mum, none of them are really interested. They are disappointed by the lack of activity from the animals, which are realistically rendered moping behind the bars. The males of the family are constantly distracted from the purpose of the visit, and as the day draws on and they become tired and hungry, they start displaying more and more animalistic behaviour themselves. Much of the time the boys are either fighting or climbing on things, and at the end of the afternoon Dad decides that the best part of the day was going home. Overall, it seems that the outing was a waste of time. That night, however, the eldest boy has a dream that he is locked in a cage at the zoo, and the final page implies that he has a kind of epiphany. The text reads, 'Do you think animals have dreams?', and the illustration shows the zoo at night, the cages silhouetted against the starry sky. The zoo

Opposite: *Piggybook*, Julia MacRae Books, 1986
Above: *Zoo*, Julia MacRae Books, 1992

animals and even the trees are encaged, but two birds can be seen flying free past the full moon.

In a way I was resurrecting my final project at art college, 'Man is an Animal', because one of the main points that I highlight in *Zoo* is the close relationship between animals and people.

The layout is consistent for the majority of the book. On the left-hand page there is an image of the human characters, painted in a cartoon-like style, with bright colours and speech bubbles complementing their clownish behaviour. In contrast, the right-hand page bears a realistic painting of the animals which confront them. Throughout the book the behaviour of the human characters is compared with that of the animals.

The boys look and behave like monkeys at all times, the mother's hair resembles the baboon's, and Dad's behaviour, at one point or another, manages to reflect most of the animal kingdom.

If you look carefully at the pictures, you will see that the background characters bear even more overt animal characteristics than the family do. The figure that takes the family's entrance money is clearly some sort of beast, and on the next page there is a variety of creatures behind the strolling protagonists. One man has a lion's tail; the woman next to him wears tiger-skin leggings; another woman wears a leopard-skin coat, and a smart man with a pig's head nonchalantly appreciates the exhibits.

As with *Hansel and Gretel*, I used the visual theme of bars throughout *Zoo*. Even when the literal bars of the cage are not actually visible, the paintings of the animals are surrounded by a thick black border which symbolizes their imprisonment. But the animals are not the only ones who are trapped.

When the family look at the orang-utan, the illustration shows them from the captive's perspective, and as they shout and bang on the glass, it looks as if *they* are the ones who are in a cage. This was intended to show how the family members are metaphorically trapped within their own dysfunctional setup.

The picture of the orang-utan is perhaps the bleakest in the book. Like many of the illustrations, it is based on a sketch that I made on one of my preparatory visits to a real zoo. The orang-utan that I saw was in exactly this wretched position. It seemed to have given up on the world, and there was something about the way it turned its back on me and the other viewers that made me feel ashamed.

Another picture that is based on a real incident is that of the tiger pacing up and down the cage. I watched a real tiger doing exactly this, and while I made sketches of it for a good half-hour it never ceased its aimless exercise. As soon as it reached one

end of the cage it would simply turn round and walk back again. The tiger was either mad, or desperately, mindlessly bored. In the book, the narrator describes the movements of the tiger in the text, but I tried to reflect them in the illustration alone.

The grass behind the beast has grown in the formation of the tiger's shape, walking in the opposite direction, and although I doubt whether many people have noticed this consciously, I like to think that it subliminally gives an impression

The bouts of anger which he occasionally displays are because he is frustrated by his own limitations. He isn't a nasty man, just incompetent.

I think the ending of Zoo is positively hopeful. The narrator has proved throughout the book that he is probably the more obnoxious of the two boys, and yet it is he who has the revelation at the end. His dream reveals a sensitivity that was not previously evident, and his newfound ability to empathize with the animals represents a significant step forward in his moral development. What seemed like a pointless trip to the zoo has in fact awakened something in his conscience, and if my intention to inspire similar thoughts from young readers about such issues is rewarded, then I see Zoo as a positive book.

It is true that the families in both Zoo and *Piggybook* have their problems, and I have been criticized

of the tiger's course back and forth across the cage.

Zoo features the first overtly religious illustration I ever painted. The gorilla's head fills the entire page, and it is divided into four by the abstract bars that form the shape of a cross. I think it is one of my best illustrations because, as well as the implied deification of the gorilla, the design of the page makes it seem that the gorilla is trapped within the book itself. Some people saw Zoo as a very bleak book. They thought I painted a cold portrait of the family, the father in particular. I disagree. I think that the father is simply trying to cope with his displacement in the role. A lot of men become fathers by accident or due to the expectations of others: they were never really cut out for the responsibility. In this instance Dad tries to compensate for his failings by telling silly jokes.

Previous spread, above, right and opposite:
Zoo, Julia MacRae Books, 1992

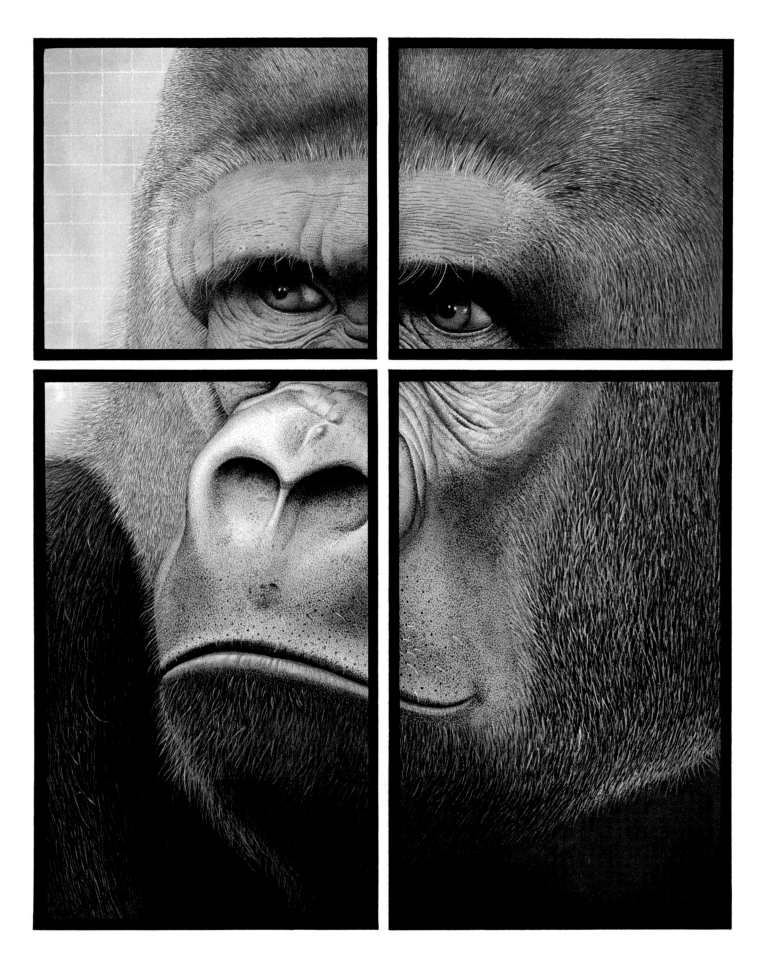

for focusing on them. It has been suggested that presenting children with a negative depiction of family life can be detrimental to the way in which they view their own families, and indeed families in general. But I think it is patronizing to assume that children are incapable of differentiating between real characters and fictional ones. Dad in *Zoo* is not a good father, but very few children would think he was modelled on their own father. Just like adults, when children read a work of fiction they see the characters within the context of that particular story. They understand that Dad exists within the context of *Zoo*, but doesn't represent all fathers in the world. Children know that most of their friends have dads, many of whom are nothing like their own – some are pleasant, some are unpleasant – and children are perfectly capable of applying this logic when they read a book. It is an ignorant adult who thinks otherwise. *Zoo* prompted a lot of criticism about my apparent string of 'bad dads'. I argued by making the same points I have just outlined, but, for all my defence, I still felt a tug to make a positive book about fathers, if only to prove that I had no agenda.

For a long time I had been wanting to write a book about my own dad, and this seemed like the perfect time to do it. I thought for a long time

about how to compose the story, but couldn't decide on a suitable approach. Then one day I found an old suitcase of my mother's. Among the photographs, birth certificates and other family documents that had been long hidden in the forgotten suitcase was Dad's old dressing gown. It was powerfully familiar, and although I had not consciously thought about it all this time, I recognized it from cameos in my books – most notably hanging from the wardrobe in *Hansel and Gretel*.

I took the dressing gown out of the case and held it, and was instantly transported back to the age of about five. For the first time in decades I remembered what it was like to be a young boy who thought his dad could do anything. It was a breakthrough, for I suddenly knew exactly how to make the book. The nostalgic effect of the dressing gown inspired me to write a story specifically about my own father and the way I felt about him as a young boy.

My Dad is a positive book about a father. With a liberal tendency to exaggerate, a young boy lists his father's virtues and abilities. The man's talents are limitless: he can do everything from jump over the moon to wrestle giants. Just like my own dad, his masculine attributes bring him success in the wrestling arena and at the fathers' race on sports day, but he also has a sensitive, artistic side that is expressed through singing, dancing and being 'as soft as a teddy'.

The dressing gown – or at least its distinctive pattern – is the visual key that links every picture, and I play the Shape Game with it throughout the book. Dad wears it constantly, be he walking the tightrope or playing football, and even when he transforms into something else – such as when he 'swims like a fish' – the pattern of the dressing gown survives in his scales.

The narrator also plays the Shape Game as he considers each simile: when Dad is 'as wise as an owl' he imagines Dad with an owl's head; a geometric diagram on the blackboard provides the illusion of a mortarboard; and, on the next page, his hairstyle resembles the bristles of the brush in his hand (and to which his daftness is compared). The book sustains this pattern until the final two pages, which bear the words, 'I love my dad. And you know what? He loves me! (And he always will.)' The last page shows Dad holding the child in a loving embrace, against a pale sunny background. It is probably the happiest picture I have ever painted.

I talk to children a lot about the background in the final image. After explaining that I could have painted the figures against a white space or a plain background in the orangy-yellow shade that is shown, I ask them why they think I included the circular, criss-cross pattern that I did. Does it remind them of anything? Answers are varied. Apart from

Opposite: *Zoo*, Julia MacRae Books, 1992
Above: *My Dad*, Doubleday, 2000

the dressing gown, the main visual theme in the book is the sun. It appears everywhere from the child's drawing behind the father on the first page to the design on the door out of which the Big Bad Wolf sullenly departs. I used the sun partly as a way of representing the warmth and light that radiate between father and child, but I was also aware of the dual meanings contained within the word sun, when interpreted phonetically.

I find that the most popular response to the final page is that the pattern of the background resembles the sun: it is as if sunlight is actually coming out of the father. Others say that it is like a tunnel; some see an echo of the pattern on the dressing gown; some arrive at the darker interpretation that it is like a spider's web – an idea that I always encourage by asking who they think is the spider and who they think is the fly. Some children think that it is like the pattern on the inside of a tree that has been cut down, and even wonder if by counting the number of rings on the 'wood grain' they can calculate the age of the father.

This experiment with children delights me because it confirms that something as seemingly arbitrary as a background pattern can inspire a huge variety of interpretations, all of which are valid, imaginative and relevant to the story.

I thought at the time that *My Dad* would be a one-off, but its tactical release around the time of Father's Day helped it to be a big seller, and in the light of this my publisher encouraged me to produce a follow-up.

Opposite: *My Dad*, Doubleday, 2000
Above: *My Mum*, Doubleday, 2005

My Mum came less easily to me. Although I based the mother in the book loosely on my own (I didn't have a material garment on which to model the dressing gown this time, but the floral design that I came up with is similar to the one which I remember her wearing), I didn't feel I had so much of a personal relationship with the character in the book. It was harder to make fun of mothers. As a father myself, I felt comfortable portraying Dad as a silly, slightly overweight show-off, but it seemed risky applying the same treatment to women, so I approached the book somewhat tentatively, taking care to make Mum more admirable than clownish. I was reasonably satisfied with the result, but I can see the self-consciousness that went into the creation of *My Mum*.

My Brother completed the trilogy. Again, the book didn't come naturally to me – to be honest, I had only ever thought the idea substantial enough

to warrant a single book – but at least this time I had some inspiration other than just the projected sales.

Unsurprisingly, I based the book on the way I had viewed my brother when I was a child, but the story was also inspired by a group of Dutch children. Before I wrote *My Brother* I went to a school in the Netherlands, and the children showed me the work they had been doing with *My Dad* and *My Mum*. They had studied the two books and subsequently produced their own version of *My Brother*. I flicked through the book they had made and was impressed by the drawings, but not surprised to see that the story was written with exactly the same formula as *My Mum* and *My Dad*. I turned to the last page, expecting the text to continue the predictable pattern which I had initiated ('I love him and he loves me too'), but they had changed the ending brilliantly. Instead of my words, they had written, 'And do you know what? I'm cool too.' I loved it, and it was just the spark of inspiration I needed to ignite enthusiasm for the project.

My Brother completes a very happy trilogy, which sums up how I *really* feel about family values.

Left: *My Mum*, Doubleday, 2005
Opposite: *My Brother*, Doubleday, 2007

I'M COOL TOO!

cool ears

cool hair

cool sweater

cool shirt

cool jeans

cool sandals

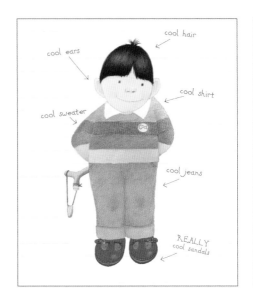

cool hair

cool ears

cool shirt

cool sweater

cool jeans

REALLY cool sandals

cool pants

and he's got MASSIVE muscles.

...he can FLY!

Yes, my brother is really COOL.

Chapter Seven
Transformations

Perhaps the most common theme in my work is that of transformation. Virtually all my books feature some sort of transformation, be it an important part of the plot, a small incident in the background, or an implied change that is woven subtly into the story. Sometimes it is the characters that seem to transform. It is quite common for a character to appear in two different incarnations during the course of the story. This is the case with the stepmother in *Hansel and Gretel*, who 'transforms' into the witch; and with the father in *Gorilla*, who 'transforms' into Hannah's ideal paternal figure. On other occasions the transformations are more explicit, such as the male characters in *Piggybook*, who literally turn into pigs.

Until 1990 I had always focused on the two opposite ends of the transformation, but when I made *Changes* I decided to concentrate on the transformation process itself.

The idea for *Changes* developed quite organically. I often have several unformed ideas floating in my head at the same time, and bringing them together creates a bigger, more meaningful idea that can be turned into a book. *Changes* was developed in this way.

The hidden details were, by now, synonymous with my work, but I was aware of their inconsequentiality. No sooner had they appeared than they would disappear again on the next page, and I had intended for a while to expand upon them and turn them into stories of their own. I allowed for this indulgence when I developed the story for *Changes*.

My mind kept settling on the image of a child looking at an object turning into another object: playing the Shape Game with his imagination. But it wasn't the two separate objects that I was interested in so much as the strange hybrid that was formed

Chapter opener: *The Tunnel*, Julia MacRae Books, 1989

Above: *Changes*, Julia MacRae Books, 1990

mid-transformation. I tried to evoke the two most disparate objects that I could think of, and imagine how they would look if they were amalgamated.

After a while, I realized that the two ideas could be combined. I had always enjoyed playing with appearance and reality in the backgrounds of my illustrations, and by forming a story around the material transformations of my preoccupation I could bring the background details to the foreground. But this wasn't enough. I needed a more substantial idea to justify the otherwise arbitrary occurrences. Thankfully, help was at hand.

Some friends had told me about a recent incident in their family. They had taken their much-loved only child to her favourite restaurant for dinner. At the end of the meal they told her some fantastic news: Mummy was going to have a baby. But instead of the happy reception they had expected, the little girl cried and cried. She already knew that from now on she would have to share her parents' affection with another child.

It was a touching story, but it was a while before I realized that I could capitalize on its poignancy. My idea was that the transformations which the protagonist sees are attributed to his parents' fore-warning of 'changes' in the family. The strange visions represent his imaginative interpretation of their mysterious prophecy. At the end of the book his parents return from the hospital with his new baby sister. So *that* was what they had meant.

I had a satisfying conclusion to the story and had settled on a premise, but I was still unsure how to approach the book. It was evident that the majority of the book would rely on the illustrations, the text very much subsidiary in this instance, so my usual method didn't seem applicable. Normally I plan a book out well in advance by developing the words and pictures together in a storyboard. This breaks down the overall design of the book into a number of scenes, which are laid out in a simple, visual format. A number of trips to London ensue, while I discuss the storyboard with my editor and, over time, we work out exactly how the words and pictures will fit together. In the case of *Changes*, the book was based on a sequence of transformations, and, apart from the pleasing denouement, I had little idea what the text would be until the images were realized. I decided to do what I had vowed not to do again since *Through the Magic Mirror*: write the story in response to the pictures.

The most persistent image in my mind was that of a kettle turning into a cat: an object which is cold, hard, metallic and inanimate turning into something with completely the opposite properties. I painted this image first. It was a series of four

pictures, each showing a different stage of the transformation, while the protagonist, Joseph, looks for clues. I treated it as an extended version of the Shape Game.

It was an excitingly new way of approaching a book. Without the limitations of a narrative, I could paint whatever I wanted: the pictures dictated the story. Like Joseph in the book, I walked around my house looking at things and imagining what they could change into. On one occasion I went into my son's bedroom and noticed a slipper on the floor. I looked at it carefully, imagined it changing into a bird, and the next moment I was painting it. It was a very enjoyable process.

I was aware of the influence of the surrealists, particularly René Magritte, throughout the production of *Changes*. One of Magritte's favourite themes was precisely this kind of transformation: he too revelled in painting subjects which were part one thing and part another. Magritte's bottles were also carrots, his boots had toes, and his fish sprouted women's legs. These images were strange, but because of the

matter-of-fact-way Magritte had painted them, there was also an air of nonchalance about them, reflecting the peculiar acceptance we have for such impossible things when we dream. Joseph accepts the bizarre transformations in much the same way.

When they warned Joseph of 'changes', his parents were referring to the new baby, but I didn't want to state this in the text until the very end of the book. Instead, I offered clues in the pictures as to what was really afoot. The clues mainly relate to the final revelation, but they also show what is really going on in Joseph's mind. Masked though they are by his imagination, his deeper concerns are about the new baby and the shift in family

Opposite and above: *Changes*, Julia MacRae Books, 1990

dynamics that it will bring about.

The clues are abundant, but subtle. Joseph's bedroom looks like Van Gogh's painting of his own sleeping quarters. Van Gogh was a notorious outsider, and the theme of alienation pervades the book. The pictures on Joseph's wall depict images of space and extraterrestrials, foreshadowing the feelings of alienation that Joseph will perhaps experience with the advent of the new arrival.

The clues accumulate. On the living room wall is a reproduction of Raphael's 'Madonna and Child', and on top of the television is a photograph of the happy family – Joseph with his father and mother, sitting on the sofa.

Opposite and left: *Changes*, Julia MacRae Books, 1990

The television shows an image of a cuckoo, and over the next few pages a significant sequence of events is played out on the screen. On the following page the frame has changed: we now see three sparrow eggs in a nest, and a much larger cuckoo egg which represents a devastating invasion. Turn over again, and the cuckoo egg has hatched. The mother sparrow – much smaller than her enormous foster offspring – does her best to feed it, but there is a notable absence of any real baby sparrows in the nest. The impostor is too big for its adopted dwelling and has forced the baby sparrows out of their home. Joseph may be concerned that he too will be usurped by the new baby. What will happen to him if the nest is too small?

In the final part of the sequence, the photograph on top of the television has an addition: a little pig has nudged itself into the image. Whatever it is that Joseph expects to arrive, he is clearly worried about its impact on the special relationship he has with his parents.

Joseph goes outside and tries to distract his troubled mind with football. But even as he holds the ball it begins to take on an oval shape. He punts it and, as it sails through the air it completes its transformation into an egg. Still airborne, the egg hatches, releasing a stork – perhaps the most traditional of symbols for birth.

A few pages later, Joseph's anxiety reaches its peak. The text at this moment simply ponders, 'Was everything going to change?' and the illustration shows Joseph leaning on a wall, looking at the twin

windows of a house. Looking back at him is what the child psychologist Gerry Byrne described as my ultimate gorilla father figure. In a dramatic image, a giant pair of gorilla eyes stares out of the windows back at Joseph, as if watching over him in his time of need. The long-established link I have made between gorillas and my father supports Byrne's theory that this gorilla represents some kind of paternal guidance from beyond the grave, but it could also be interpreted as a reinforcement of the deification that I sometimes apply to the great ape. There is definitely a God-like quality to the enormous eyes that return Joseph's gaze, and, although I painted it for the power of the image alone, I can understand why much has been read into the illustration.

Fed up with all the changes, Joseph goes back to his room, closes the door and turns off the light. The left-hand illustration shows him in the final stages of closing the door, and, in the tiny sliver of darkness that remains on the other side, a mysterious shape is faintly visible. If we look closely, we can just make out an eye in the gloom. It would seem that a ghostly figure is trying to get in. The phantom's apparent desire to intrude on Joseph's space would suggest that it is yet another symbol of the imminent infant invasion, but there is also something of Joseph's own reflection in its form. Could it be that Joseph is concerned he will be replaced, or even duplicated? Another Joseph. What would that mean?

When the door opens again, Joseph's mother and father come in with the new baby. All is revealed.

Opposite, above and below:
Changes, Julia MacRae Books, 1990

The final page bears a small illustration of the whole family sitting together on the sofa. Joseph sits between his mother and father, holding the baby. The text reads, 'This is your sister.'

The image echoes that of the photograph on top of the television, and the smiling faces suggest that all the characters are just as happy as before. Everything is all right. Joseph, his mother and father all have their own individual mugs on the ground

beside them – a detail that unites the three of them and reassures Joseph that nothing is really going to change. Rather than being a threat to the family equilibrium, the baby is a joyful addition.

Changes was the first book to make the theme of transformation its prevailing subject, but it was by no means unfamiliar territory for me. Not long before *Changes*, I had illustrated *Alice's Adventures in Wonderland*, a book that also deals extensively with transformations.

There are many reasons why Carroll's classic text has always fascinated me, not least its fairytale-like quality and surrealist overtones, and it is unsurprising that the experience of illustrating *Alice* had a powerful effect on my work for a considerable time afterwards. The surfacing of Carrollesque themes in *Changes* was in fact the result of a lingering influence, for the book that is chronologically flanked by these two could also be described as a 'post-*Alice*' text. The heroine's venture down the rabbit hole was probably one of the main ideas behind the creation of *The Tunnel*.

I had been wanting to illustrate a fairy tale for a while, but although *Hansel and Gretel* was by now a distantly bygone project, I didn't feel ready to revisit a classic. I preferred to draw on an array of fairy tales with a view to creating my own.

The motif of a tunnel was the perfect starting point. Lewis Carroll cast the rabbit hole as the gateway to Wonderland, and he wasn't the only one to exploit its symbolism. The tunnel has been a constant icon in the history of children's fiction. Besides Carroll's rabbit hole, the idea of a portal to 'wonderland' is manifested in C. S. Lewis's wardrobe; the hidden door to Frances Hodgson Burnett's secret garden; even Doctor Who's TARDIS.

Tunnels also carry a great deal of personal significance for me. One of my most vivid memories from childhood is crawling along the tunnel that was dug into the wall of the 'bottomless' well at Crows Nest Park. Although there was nothing at the end, the fairy tales I had read ensured that the sense of danger extended beyond the obvious dimensional hazards and into the realms of goblins and witchcraft. It was terrifying but exciting, and tunnels have retained these strangely complementary qualities for me ever since.

Another memorable tunnel-like structure from my childhood is the viaduct that stood in the grounds of the Red Lion. Although it wasn't at the front of my mind when I created *The Tunnel*, it perhaps played a part in the conception of the idea. I did not mention before that the ground beyond the viaduct was strictly out-of-bounds to my brother and me. I was never quite sure what was so dangerous about the unremarkable fields on the other side, but our parents' confidence in their unnamed perils assigned to the viaduct the identity of a gateway to the unknown. It marked the limits of our domain, and the nondescript grassland was merely the beginning of the vast territory which we knew simply as 'the outside world'. To the fledglings that we were, the viaduct was as likely to announce the entrance to hell as it was the outskirts of Halifax.

The Tunnel is about a brother and sister, who are 'not at all alike'. While Rose is quiet, introverted and imaginative, preferring to read her book of fairy tales than do anything more physical, Jack is tough, extroverted and sporty, and wouldn't be seen dead with anything more literary than a football. Rose's efforts to sleep at night are disturbed by her brother's nocturnal antics. He knows that she is afraid of the dark, so he creeps into her room wearing a wolf mask to scare her.

One morning their mother forces them to go out and play together. They have nothing in common, and are bored with each other's company in minutes. But things perk up for Jack when he discovers a mysterious tunnel. Rose is scared and stays on the outside, but Jack crawls in. She waits and waits, but when he doesn't return she eventually decides to go in after him. She abandons her book in the mouth of the tunnel and crawls inside.

Rose emerges in a quiet wood, but there is no sign of Jack. As she walks on, the pleasant environment quickly becomes a dark, scary forest, and her thoughts turn to wolves, giants and witches. She works herself into a frenzy of terror and breaks into a run. Emerging from the forest into a clearing, Rose sees a terrible thing. Jack is there in front of her, but he has been turned to stone.

'Oh no!' she sobs. 'I'm too late.' She throws her arms around the statue and weeps. Gradually, the effect of her embrace causes the stone to soften and grow warm, until eventually her brother is restored to life. He returns her hug.

They walk home together, and when their mother asks if everything is all right, Jack and Rose smile knowingly at each other.

Although *The Tunnel* is, on an immediate level, about a brother and a sister, Jack and Rose represent two sides of the same person. Jack is the 'masculine' side: loud and outgoing, physically active and ready to rush into any situation in a manner that is as brave as it is irresponsible. Rose is the 'feminine' side: calm and imaginative, thoughtful, sensitive. Although she thinks carefully before acting, she can allow her fears and emotions to get the better of her. I reinforced this idea with the endpapers and the backgrounds against which the children stand in the opening portraits. Rose is depicted in front of some floral wallpaper; Jack, in front of a brick wall. I remembered the question Aidan Chambers asked on the BBC programme all those years ago, that I had been unable to answer at the time. Finally I had delivered a significant brick wall!

The backgrounds appear to be as different as

they can possibly be – the hard, robust bricks contrasting dramatically with the soft flowery wall-paper. But if you look at the endpapers closely you can see the vertical lines which reveal the adjoining sheets on both designs. The bricks are also part of the wallpaper. Although the two halves appear to be very different, they are in fact part of the same overall design: male and female; yin and yang.

The characters in the book are partly based on my brother and me. We weren't completely differ-ent, but we did fight a lot. Although we were both physical and sporty, I was younger and more emotionally vulnerable than Michael, and he (like any older brother) sometimes took advantage of this by trying to upset or scare me. While he was stronger and more outgoing, I was the one who had to check under my bed every night, and, although I would never have admitted it at the time, I was certainly more suited to Rose's floral background than he! But Michael had his sensitive moments, and I could be tough when I wanted to be, so in many ways we were very similar.

This is the case in *The Tunnel*. Rose is 'masculine' enough to venture into the tunnel and rescue her brother, while Jack demonstrates sufficient 'femininity' to be softened by a loving embrace. *The Tunnel* is ultimately about understanding that both parts of the masculine/feminine dichotomy are present in all our constitutions.

The Tunnel is full of references to fairy tales. When Jack tries to frighten Rose in the night, it appears that her bedroom is a shrine to the Brothers Grimm. On the wall is a Walter Crane illustration from *Red Riding Hood*, and hanging from the wardrobe is a hooded coat of an appropriate shade. Beside the bed is a night-light in the shape of a house, designed to look like it is made from something other than bricks: gingerbread, perhaps? Jack, in his wolf mask, enters the room on hands and knees. The shadow that he casts on the floor is in the shape of an archway, foreshadowing the tunnel that is soon to arrive. The arch shape is also reminiscent of a viaduct.

Rose is surrounded by fairytale references in the

forest. The strange shapes in the trees were not pre-planned. I painted them using a very fluid, loose watercolour technique, allowing the paints to run into each other and create a myriad of interesting shapes. I played the Shape Game with the patterns that formed, turning them into more recognizable symbols. In the first of the forest illustrations there is a thumb in the tree on the right, and a discarded basket in its roots. Dangling from the thumb is a rope that leads inside the tree, but what lurks at the bottom? Perhaps it is a dog with eyes the size of saucers. Focusing on the basket, it appears that something round has spilled out: it must be a cake for Grandma. In the background, on the right, a fire has been lit, but there is no sign of the two abandoned children who are responsible; nor of their father, the woodcutter, who has left his axe in the foreground. Behind the trees, some unidentified greenery stretches heavenward: who would have thought that a handful of beans could spawn such a prodigious plant?

On the next page, Rose sprints past a different set of trees. This time the creatures in the woodwork are as palpable as they are terrifying. From the tree on the left emerges a monstrous duo. An armless Daddy Bear snarls as he threatens to burst from the roots, accompanied by the tusked head of Beauty's Beast. The latter is again based on a Walter Crane depiction – something between a bear and a wild boar.

Embedded in the tree on the right is the wolf. Dressed in his proverbial sheep's clothing, his pose echoing the Crane illustration that we saw earlier on Rose's bedroom wall, he watches with sinister composure as Red Riding Hood races past.

In the background, the gingerbread house offers its sugary allure, and I have employed the same visual clue that I did for *Hansel and Gretel*: the gap in the curtains forms a significant black triangle.

Jack's petrification has many cultural sources. Human beings being turned to stone is a narrative tradition that encompasses fairy tales, mythology and classic children's literature. Although I consulted nothing at the time, I suspect that C. S. Lewis's *The Lion, the Witch and the Wardrobe* was an influence, as was Medusa from Greek mythology. And, yet again, Magritte should also be credited for his several paintings on the subject.

Jack and Rose are united at the end of the book.

They have survived the experience together, and their affection for one another is cemented by the smile they share on the last page. The final endpaper reinforces their unity further. The combined brick and flower designs of the wallpaper, coupled with the football and fairytale book that lie together in the bottom right-hand corner, renew the implication that they represent two sides of the same person, and also ensures that the story continues beyond the obvious 'ending'.

Previous spread, left and below:
The Tunnel, Julia MacRae Books, 1989

Chapter Eight

Every Picture Tells a Story

When children ask me how to draw I usually tell them to look extremely carefully. To me, this is the most important skill for an artist. The great artists are those who view the world with their eyes truly open and have the ability to *really* look at everything they see.

As a society, we undervalue the power of sight. Although we have been blessed with excellent optical abilities, one constantly hears people lamenting the 'visual society' we have become, and we are told from childhood not to 'judge a book by its cover'. But I believe that you can tell a lot about something just from looking at it. Some of the best portraits are those in which the character of the sitter has been rendered transparent, simply by the nuances of expression. A good painter can expose the model's spirit so completely that it is impossible for the viewer not to draw conclusions about his or her character. Rather than the tool of a rude or judgemental attitude, I see the discerning eye as a vital aid in the production of meaningful art.

I also think it is important for painters to look at paintings as often as they can. Just as writers learn much about the art of shaping a text by reading great books, or jazz musicians learn to improvise firstly by copying the licks of their heroes, painters too should look to the works of the masters for guidance and inspiration. Great paintings have been massively influential to me, both technically and in terms of stoking my imagination.

It is a testament to its profundity that the phrase, 'Every picture tells a story' has become such a cliché. My favourite paintings are those that have a definite story behind them, be it an epic representation of a historical event, such as Géricault's 'The Raft of the Medusa', or a more subtle, narratively cryptic scene such as 'Nighthawks' by Edward Hopper. Such masterpieces have greatly enhanced my skills both as a painter and as a writer.

The tendency to reference or even reproduce paintings has become something of a trademark in my work. When scanning my illustrations, it is quite common to spot a Van Dyck hanging on the wall, or a Gainsborough perched above the fireplace. They are usually employed as a narrative aid – the paintings are carefully chosen to shadow the plot of the story – but they are also there as a homage to my influences. I love paintings, and why not share this with my young readers? It is a fantasy of mine that children might appreciate a great painting all the more because they recognize it from one of my books.

Both *The Tunnel* and *Changes* feature numerous references: references to paintings, to other stories, to the natural world. Referencing was becoming a habit, and I suppose it was only a matter of time before I made a book that was dominated by cultural allusions.

I made *Willy the Dreamer* in 1997, at a very troublesome point in my career. I had been working on another book – *Voices in the Park* – and was about halfway through when I was struck by a tremendous sense of doubt about my future. I was painting a scene that takes place in the depths of winter, from the point of view of a man who is very depressed, and the effect of the bleak winter scene seemed to symbolize my diminishing confidence in the book. I went into a bookshop and surveyed

what appeared to be an abyss of cuddly toys, CD-ROMs and books about cute TV tie-in characters. I felt as if I was working in the wrong place at the wrong time. I was producing a re-working of an old book – an indulgence that I didn't think the times would allow me – and had this sudden conviction that I would never see *Voices in the Park* in this shop, or any other.

I decided to have a break from children's books . . . perhaps even give them up entirely. I had been making books for half my life and hadn't a clue what to do instead; all I knew was that it had to involve making art. If I carried on painting, maybe I would find an answer. So I did what I hadn't done since childhood: I painted for the sheer love of painting, creating whatever I liked with neither limitations nor purpose. I reclaimed my zest for art and was thrilled by the sense of emancipation, my brush flitting across the paper with a playfulness I had forgotten I was capable of, but when I looked at the three or four paintings I had made with this new approach, I noticed something curious. There was something missing. Every painting had a strong sense of narrative, and all they lacked was the accompanying text. They were illustrations. I had made the paintings in the hope that they would lead me somewhere, and they did: straight back to the path I had followed for twenty-five years. The reason I had made picture books for so long was because I loved it, and it suddenly seemed ridiculous to think of doing anything else.

The time out from children's books may not

have led to anything new, but it was by no means a useless period. I really enjoyed the process of painting without the restrictions of the narrative, and this made me wonder if there was any way I could adopt this free approach to illustration in my picture books, without detracting from their readability.

The American illustrator Chris Van Allsburg had managed it. His *The Mysteries of Harris Burdick* is an extraordinary, unique picture book with a brilliant premise. The fictional introduction – the only piece of text longer than two sentences – explains that the pictures in the book are the articles of an unsolved mystery. Thirty years ago a man called Harris Burdick approached a children's book publisher, explaining that he had written fourteen stories. Rather than burden the publisher with his entire body of work, he brought just one picture from each story, under each of which he had written the title and a brief caption for the illustration. The publisher was fascinated by the pictures and told Burdick that he would like to see the stories in their entirety as soon as possible. Burdick agreed to bring them to him the next day. But he didn't show up. For years, the publisher tried desperately to track him down without success. Harris Burdick had mysteriously disappeared and all that was left of him was the fourteen mesmerizing pictures.

The rest of the book shows us the strange black and white pencil illustrations with their titles and captions. Each one is a superb work of art. Besides

Chapter opener: *Willy's Pictures,* Walker Books, 2000

Above: 'Under the Rug' from *The Mysteries of Harris Burdick,* Houghton Mifflin Harcourt, Chris Van Allsburg, 1984

being brilliantly drawn, they are impossibly imaginative. I am in awe of the work, and I admire Van Allsburg for his accomplishment. Having set himself up with the inspired introduction, he was then at liberty to produce a series of drawings entirely from his imagination, free from the limitations of a traditional narrative. The result is a series of implied narratives that are as enthralling as the child's imagination chooses them to be. I have talked about the importance of leaving gaps between the pictures and the text for children to fill in with their own imaginations. In the case of *The Mysteries of Harris Burdick*, the gaps are cavernous.

The book was a favourite of my own children, who were thrilled, enchanted and frightened by the pictures in equal measure. One image in particular was such a powerful stimulus for Joe's imagination that it kept him awake at night. The title of the Harris Burdick story is 'Under the Rug', and the illustration shows an angry, frightened man raising a chair above his head, preparing to strike a mysterious lump under the rug. The caption reads, 'Two weeks passed and it happened again'. Joe didn't know what the thing under the rug was, but he worked himself into a frenzy considering the possibilities. I tried to explain that it was only a picture, but it was shallow rhetoric: I knew that the words offered no comfort to an imaginative child. In the end I decided to draw 'the solution'. I showed Joe my interpretation of the following scene, in which the man replaces the chair on the floor as a tiny kitten emerges from under the rug. It seemed to do the trick.

I didn't expect to match the ingenuity of *The Mysteries of Harris Burdick*, but hoped that I could emulate the balance between artistic freedom and reader satisfaction that Van Allsburg had achieved.

There were no fully realized ideas in my mind at this time; all I knew was that I wanted to make a book about dreams. Dreams are a subject that many artists find fascinating. This is largely because when we dream we enter the kind of hyper-imaginative version of reality that artists strive to conceive in a waking state. I certainly have a broader capacity for creativity when I am asleep, and I wish there was a way of effectively evoking in art the unique experience of dreaming. Countless artists have tried, but, as much as I admire the dream-inspired work of the surrealists, I cannot say that a great many have succeeded.

To dream is to play an advanced version of the Shape Game. The shapes are our memories of the real waking world: quotidian experiences and images stored in our subconscious. When we sleep, our minds play the Shape Game with this material and turn it into the fantastic scenarios which we associate only with dreaming.

Alternatively, the process could be viewed as a reversal of the Shape Game. When we dream, we take on the same view of the world that the surrealists did. Recognizable symbols from the real world are assembled in a seemingly haphazard way, creating extraordinary juxtapositions and impossible chains of events that are far more interesting than the isolated components. In a way, we are taking the final, 'changed' image from the Shape Game and reducing it to its original state of abstraction, removing any certainty from the symbol and reclaiming its original ambiguity. Like the initial shape, the incoherence and unpredictability of dreams give them a naive quality, which ties in with the surrealists' endeavours to retrieve the child's way of looking at the world.

These thoughts had always attracted me to make a book about dreams, but the requirements of the assumed story had deterred me until now. As fascinating as my own dreams are, the word 'narrative' can be applied to them in only the loosest sense. To illustrate a typical night in my life would be to produce a work that is as fragmented as it is horrifying: a picture-book version of free writing; a world in which a short vest is the only defence against my total lack of dignity! Undesirable images aside, I knew it would be difficult, if not impossible, to achieve a linear narrative from the surreal, unrelated series of happenings that typically form my dreams. Besides, I was looking to break away from the shackles of my usual plot-dictated approach. I was fed up with painting endless intermediary pictures, necessitated purely by the demands of the narrative.

What I really wanted was to produce a series of pictures, each of which illustrated a different dream. But I wasn't in a position to simply paint

Opposite: *Willy the Dreamer*, Walker Books, 1997

what I wanted; nor was I foolish enough to forget the fact that children's books are my livelihood. Each time I put brush to paper it is ultimately my professional responsibility to produce a commodity. So how was I to turn a series of dreams into a saleable children's book?

In the end I decided not to worry about it. If I concentrated on painting the pictures in my usual style, I would perhaps create a number of stories within each illustration; hopefully their abundance and intrigue would warrant the absence of a through-running narrative.

Due to a combination of my affection for the character and a desire to increase the appeal of a book that could otherwise be viewed as a self-indulgent venture, I turned once again to Willy for the protagonist. By this stage Willy had enjoyed multiple outings, in various guises. So far he had appeared as a wimp, a champ and a wizard: could he not be a dreamer also? His dreams are strange and varied. Amid the dreams of flight and, conversely, those of being physically unable to run from a faceless chaser (although, in Willy's case, the pursuer bears the outline of Buster Nose), are more poignant scenarios, such as when Willy dreams that he is a street beggar.

In many of the dreams he imagines himself in contrasting roles and professions. In one dream he is a sumo wrestler; in the next he is a ballet dancer. Tonight he is a famous writer; tomorrow he will be a scuba diver.

Most of the dreams have references to popular

culture, many of which allude to dreams themselves. Willy's very first dream is that 'he's a film star',
but in the illustration he is depicted as several,
including Frankenstein's monster (the dream of a
disturbed scientist); all three of Dorothy's needy
Oz-inhabiting companions (who are, it transpires,
the products of a dream); and King Kong. On an
immediate level, Kong, as a commodity, is the
dream of the money-hungry Karl Denham, but he is
also, by extension, a symbol of the American Dream.

The references continue throughout the book.
After being a film star, Willy dreams that he is a
generic 'singer', but the illustration puts forward a
strong argument for him being Elvis Presley. As
a famous writer, Willy is surrounded by characters
from Lewis Carroll's *Alice* novels; and, as an

explorer, who should he discover watching
television in the jungle but the writer of the
ultimate masterwork on dreams, Sigmund Freud.
But the most prolific references are to famous
paintings. Freud's jungle is quite obviously based
on Henri Rousseau's. With Buster Nose in pursuit,
the landscape that Willy tries unsuccessfully to
traverse is based on De Chirico's 'The Uncertainty
of the Poet'. All at sea, the mermaid to whom
Willy extends his helpful pole is a substitute for
'The Glove' in Max Ernst's series of etchings about
the dream of an obsessive romantic.

The link between dreams and the surrealists was
impossible for me to ignore. The sky in Willy's
dream of flight is straight after Dali; it is the same
artist's 'The Persistence of Memory' that inspires the

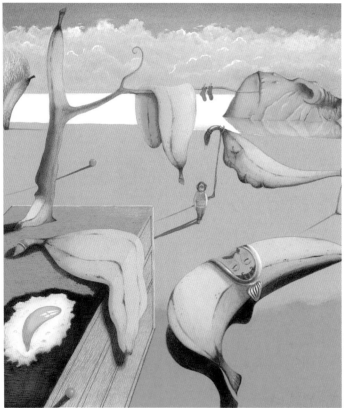

Opposite, above and overleaf:
Willy the Dreamer, Walker Books, 1997

'strange landscape' through which the chimp wanders at one point; and Magritte is referenced throughout. Ay, there's the rub! A fascination with the paintings of René Magritte has always been evident in my work, and my enthusiasm for the great surrealist made the events that occurred in the aftermath of *Willy the Dreamer* all the more infuriating. Soon after the book was published, my French publisher received a letter from the Magritte Estate, claiming that I had totally infringed copyright laws.

There are Magritte references at several points in the book – most blatantly when Willy dreams that he is a painter (an illustration in which no fewer than six Magritte paintings are displayed with notable banana alterations), and when he dreams that he sees a 'fierce monster' reflected in the mirror (twenty years after *Through the Magic Mirror*, the image is another reminder of my attraction to one of the Belgian's simplest paintings, 'Not to Be Reproduced') – but the illustration that the Magritte Estate objected to more than any other was the very first one. It shows Willy sitting in an armchair; on the wall behind him is a reproduction of 'The Castle in the Pyrenees'. It is a beguiling image, and I see no reason why Willy – imaginative and aesthetically discerning chimp that he is – wouldn't decide to have it on his wall, but I chose it mainly because of its symbolism. The painting introduces us to the world of dreaming by presenting the well-known dream symbol of a castle in the air. Magritte was a dream enthusiast, and his connection with the book always seemed appropriate.

The Magritte Estate employs lawyers to check for cultural references to René Magritte. The whole of *Willy the Dreamer* must have been too much for them, but what really pushed them to pounce was this little image. Whereas the other references are all altered in some way, the painting on Willy's wall is a direct copy of a Magritte work, albeit a much scaled-down, watercolour one. This was the crux of their argument, but it turned out that all the Magritteisms in the book were sufficiently immoderate to infringe copyright. The law states that if a considerable portion of a painting is copied, then, unless the artist has been dead for more than seventy-five years, permission must be sought before publishing. The Estate demanded that all copies be taken off the shelves and that either Walker (the publisher of this particular book) or I pay them a lot of money. Thankfully Walker sorted out the monetary matter, and we eventually managed to negotiate that all the existing copies could be sold. If we wanted to sell any reprints or paperbacks, however, then the Magritte references had to be omitted. Walker were keen to print the book in paperback, and consequently there are two versions of *Willy the Dreamer*: the 'guilty', Magritte-heavy version and the 'reprieved' one with the references painted out.

At first I felt terrible about the whole matter. The accusatory nature of the Estate's approach made it seem that I was being exposed as a cheat; it was as if I had been caught stealing from Magritte in some way. But after reflection I realized this wasn't true at all. All artists have a right not to have their work copied, but my intention was as a homage. *Willy the Dreamer* is a book about dreams: I referenced Magritte because there is probably no other artist in history whose body of work is more explicitly dream-inspired. Far from trying to exploit Magritte's paintings, I was in fact trying to promote them. I was presenting great art to children in a way that I hoped would make it more accessible to them. *Willy the Dreamer* is often used in schools as a vehicle for discussing art – comparing and contrasting my versions with the originals – and before the fiasco I would have thought that an organization dedicated to preserving Magritte's appeal would find this as pleasing as I do. Magritte often borrowed images from existing paintings – one by Manet and another by David – and adapted them by substituting the human figures with coffins. I applied exactly the same process to Magritte's paintings, only I used bananas in place of his pipes, apples and baguettes. When I painted these images, it didn't occur to me that I should feel guilty, and, in the same way, I doubt that Magritte considered himself to be stealing from Manet and David when he reinterpreted their paintings. If anything it is a sign of respect to Manet and David that they were able to provide Magritte with inspiration. In *Willy the Dreamer* I did exactly what Magritte and thousands of other painters have

done throughout the history of art: played the Shape Game with existing paintings.

Before I started on the revised version, Walker arranged for a lawyer to go through the book and produce a page-by-page breakdown of exactly where and how I had infringed the copyright. We weren't prepared to take any risks, so we made sure he considered every picture; not just those that referenced Magritte. The breakdown proved to be quite extensive, and at first I was annoyed at having to make so many changes, but in the end I quite enjoyed altering the pictures; playing the Shape Game with my own illustrations. Some of the pictures required considerable alterations, and for these I made entire new watercolour paintings. For other paintings in which the references were few or small, I worked with my original illustrations, painting over the offending details in gouache. This was the case for all the Magritte images. I changed the pattern of the waves on the cover so that the sea no longer resembled that in 'The Castle in the Pyrenees'. It was this painting, of course – referenced again in the opening illustration – which ignited the controversy in the first place. In the new version, I replaced the reproduction that hangs on Willy's wall with an image of a neutral seascape.

When Willy dreams of being a famous painter, instead of filling his studio with his interpretations of Magritte paintings, he instead looks to Van Gogh for inspiration. Having ascertained that Van Gogh was out of copyright, I guiltlessly set about substituting Magritte's 'Not to Be Reproduced' with Van Gogh's

'Sunflowers'; the surrealist's 'The Son of Man' with the post-impressionist's 'Chair'. It was actually quite good fun.

Other artists posed no problem because they were out of copyright. The heavily Rousseau-influenced jungle that Willy 'explores' was allowed to stay because the artist had been dead for more than seventy-five years, as was the *Alice* illustration, which is clearly based on the original drawings by the sufficiently deceased Sir John Tenniel.

Once I had changed all the pictures the lawyer advised, Walker made proofs of the new version and sent them to the experts for a legal assessment. They assured us that the book complied with British copyright laws, but that other countries' stricter systems might still object to certain images. This exasperated me. I couldn't be bothered to change the illustrations again, and I was all for abandoning the paperback release. But Walker Books sent the new proofs to the Magritte Estate anyway, along with an accompanying letter which explained exactly what I was trying to do, stressing the point that my intentions were to celebrate Magritte and make his paintings more accessible to children. They took this into account and approved the new version. This seemed like a major triumph, and the go-ahead from the Magritte Estate revived our confidence, providing enough of an incentive to resume the production of the paperbacks. *Willy the Dreamer* was restored to the shelves and the nightmare was over.

But there was another issue at stake. *Willy the Dreamer* represented a new approach to picture books for me. It seemed I had finally found a way of abandoning the linear narrative: I could paint what I liked. *Willy the Dreamer* was the most enjoyable picture book to work on in years, and I was infected by the freedom that was suddenly available to me. Furthermore, in the state of blissful ignorance I had enjoyed before the legal matters, the opportunity to reference my favourite paintings had made the process even sweeter. In the period between finishing *Willy the Dreamer* and the trouble with the Magritte Estate, I was so enthused by the new approach that I started another *Willy* book in a similar vein, only *even more* reliant on famous paintings. *Willy's Pictures* is presented to look like Willy's own sketchbook, and every page bears his interpretation of a great work of art. In other words, whereas the offending references in *Willy the Dreamer* were shrouded, albeit thinly, by the context of Willy's dreams, *Willy's Pictures* offered no excuses whatsoever. After the Magritte Estate's intervention, I realized that the new book might as well be called *Willy the Exploiter* or *Willy's Copyright Infringements*.

Naturally, the *Willy the Dreamer* debacle was a huge kick in the teeth because I knew that not one but two books were under threat. If the production of *Willy the Dreamer* was such a scandal, then *Willy's Pictures* would surely be the Watergate of children's picture books!

Nevertheless, I was having such fun making the book that I resigned myself to the troubles ahead. I knew that I would have to scrap some of the pictures I had already painted, and that a long,

arduous legal battle dominated the horizon, but I decided to go through with it anyway.

The inspiration for the book came to me in Chicago. I was on an exhausting trip to a suburb of the windy city – an unattractive part of town where everything around me was grey and uninspiring, and I had reached a point where the whole trip was starting to feel like a miserable ordeal. I was bored by the sound of my own voice and, having been into libraries every day, reeling out the same words again and again, it was a great relief when I was finally given a day off. I went into the heart of the city and visited the Art Institute of Chicago. Suddenly all the greyness of the trip evaporated. I was

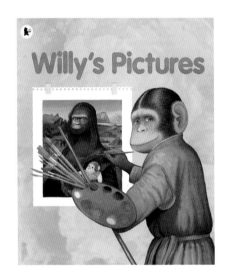

surrounded by colour and magic. Everywhere I looked there was a brilliant work of art that I had only ever seen in reproduction and, as I marvelled at one after the other, the whole trip suddenly seemed worthwhile.

One of the pictures that stood out was 'American Gothic' by Grant Wood. It is a brilliant double portrait of an aged farming couple. Even though the sitters for the portrait were foreign to the ways of agriculture – the man is Wood's dentist; the woman, his sister – it is an extraordinary character study, beautifully painted. I looked at the picture for a long time, and the more I looked, the more this couple reminded me of another. Gazing at the stark expressions on their beautiful, wizened faces, I saw my favourite chimps, Willy and Millie, married and grown old together. It struck me as a good starting point for a picture book, and I started to ruminate there and then. *Willy's Pictures* could be a collection of Willy's artwork: a series of studies in which he depicts himself in the context of iconic paintings like 'American Gothic'. The book would be varied (I could choose paintings from a variety of different genres); educational (I could even have reproductions of the originals at the back of the book which children could compare with Willy's versions); and fun (in some of the pictures Willy could appear comically incongruous or lost, and there could be jokes throughout). I was instantly very excited about the idea and set about turning it into a book as soon as I got back from Chicago.

The first painting I made was the 'American Gothic' illustration. It was the painting that gave me the idea for the book in the first place, and it will always be my favourite of Willy's pictures, even though it didn't appear in the final publication.

The results of the legal enquiry proved to be as mixed as we had expected. Some of the estates were comfortable with the project and allowed me to reference the artists without restriction, while others denied me any rights whatsoever. To my great disappointment, the Grant Wood Estate was one of the latter. It was particularly frustrating because

'American Gothic' is a painting that has been referenced hundreds of times in a vast array of contexts, by very different artists. So numerous and diverse are its offspring that the Chicago Institute held an exhibition in their honour. For some reason, however, I wasn't allowed to continue the trend.

So Walker Books and I went through the same process we had with *Willy the Dreamer*. Lawyers were contacted, as were the necessary estates for the artists I had referenced, and once we found out which illustrations were unacceptable I set about repainting the pictures. Several of the illustrations couldn't be used at all, because the relevant estates wouldn't allow it. Willy's private sketchbook actually extends beyond the paintings displayed in the final publication, and among those that couldn't be printed are versions of Picasso, Chagall and Max Ernst paintings.

But thankfully most of the illustrations were cleared. Several of the artists, including Botticelli and Vermeer, had been dead long enough for the copyright to have expired, and some of the estates, such as those representing Edward Hopper and Frida Kahlo, were happy for the illustrations to be printed regardless.

Many of the paintings referenced in *Willy's Pictures* are among my favourites, but this isn't the only reason I chose them. As with *Willy the Dreamer*, it was important that the paintings could be turned into stories, and in the absence of a traditional narrative it was necessary for the pictures to make up a series of micro-stories which children could engage with. They also had to accommodate Willy in a variety of funny, mysterious and imaginative ways, and it was Willy's inclusion in the paintings that accounted for much of the book's humour. For example, I recognized that to be thrust into a typical Ingres painting would be an embarrassing ordeal for the shy chimp, so, in a take on Ingres's 'The Turkish Bath', I painted Willy fleeing from the female changing room at the swimming pool, mortified by his mistake.

In his nightmarish version of Van Eyck's 'The Arnolfini Marriage', Willy depicts himself in the foreground, emitting a Munch-like scream, racked with anguish as Millie and Buster Nose are joined in holy matrimony. Every picture has its own story, with Willy at the centre. The only text in the book is the title of each painting and a caption, much like Van Allsburg's *The Mysteries of Harris Burdick*. *Willy's Pictures* is meant to be a testament to the storytelling quality of great paintings, and I like to imagine that children obtain as much pleasure from reading the stories presented in the illustrations as they do from reading a more conventional picture book.

Some of the original paintings are examples of the Shape Game themselves. Max Ernst took an image of a Sudanese corn bin, and turned it into a strange elephant in his painting 'Elephant Celebes'. I took the game a stage further, by turning Ernst's

Previous spread: *Willy's Pictures*, Walker Books, 2000

Right: *Willy's Pictures*, Walker Books, 2000

elephant into a robot vacuum cleaner with the head of Buster Nose, and his headless manikin into Willy.

Leonardo da Vinci was also a fan of the Shape Game. There is a famous piece of advice that he gave to his students. He told them to look at an old wall; if they looked long and hard enough, they would see in its cracks and blemishes landscapes, monsters, battles and the whole world. I took his advice. I studied da Vinci's painting 'Mona Lisa' very carefully until I saw all sorts of things in the background. In Willy's version of 'Mona Lisa', I painted what I saw. Researching *Willy's Pictures* confirmed what I already knew: artists have played the Shape Game throughout history.

I was particularly pleased with my idea to present the original paintings at the back of the book. My initial intention was to have the originals reproduced the same size as Willy's pictures, and to present them on consecutive pages, so that the child looks first at Willy's version and then turns the page to see the painting that inspired him. But the designers at Walker told me this wasn't practical, the main reason being that it would double the size of the book. In the end we made the last page into a foldout. The originals are presented as small, thumbnail images, with the titles and Willy's descriptions underneath or beside them. I wanted it to be a game – a bit like a spot-the-difference puzzle – for children to compare the originals with Willy's versions and see how he has changed them. I suppose the idea is to dissect the results of Willy's Shape Game.

Although neither book is a conventional story about an event in Willy's life, I think that both *Willy the Dreamer* and *Willy's Pictures* tell us a lot about my most popular character. Both books feature subtle clues about the nature of Willy's 'existence' – *Willy's Pictures* with Willy sitting at a table, working on his version of Botticelli's 'The Birth of Venus', a reproduction of the original beside him. In the context of fiction, Willy is doing exactly what I was in reality: playing the Shape Game with a painting to create 'Willy's' interpretation. What, or who, does this make Willy? I have received many letters from children asking if Willy is based on me, and I think that *Willy's Pictures* goes some way to answering this question. The last illustration shows a figure that could be Willy walking away from the same table that we saw at the beginning of the book. The figure is halfway out of the door, so his face is concealed, but among the items he has left in the

work area are Willy's trademark sleeveless pullover and a chimpanzee mask.

Equally mysterious is the unidentified human portrait that Willy is painting on the cover. The original cover of the book bears two names, and they are as interchangeable as the two faces which are also represented. The painting to which Willy applies the finishing touches is effectively a self-portrait.

The last page of *Willy the Dreamer* is perhaps even more philosophical. Willy is shown sitting in the same armchair that he was at the beginning, but there are a number of differences. For a start, I have played my usual tricks with the minutiae of the illustration. The flowers that patterned the wallpaper

Opposite, top: *Mona Lisa*, Leonardo da Vinci, 1503-1506
Opposite, bottom: *Willy's Pictures*, Walker Books, 2000
Above, left: *The Birth of Venus*, Sandro Botticelli, c.1486
Above, right: *Willy's Pictures*, Walker Books, 2000

in the opening picture have transformed into an arrangement of Willy heads, each sporting a different hat, and the rock in the painting on the wall also bears the chimp's grinning face. But look closely at Willy himself. The text reads, 'Willy dreams', but his left eye is clearly open, and he appears to be winking directly at the reader. If you look carefully, you can see that the lines of the seat are visible on Willy's trousers, as if he is painted onto the chair. This detail reminds us that Willy is part of the painting. He is imaginary; he doesn't exist. *Ceci n'est pas une pipe*. Willy dreams, but so does the reader; so does the author. Willy *is* a dream . . .

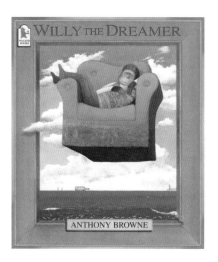

Opposite and above: *Willy the Dreamer*, Walker Books, 1997
Right: *Willy's Pictures*, Walker Books, 2000

Chapter Nine

A Way of Working

Until now I have talked mainly about the ideas, problems and strategies that have been specific to certain books. It is true that I have experimented with a variety of approaches to the process throughout my career, but the majority of my books have been created with a similar formula.

It always starts with the idea. The most successful ideas are those that come to me organically, and I have learned over the years that to consciously try and pluck an idea from nowhere is a futile strategy. Sitting down and searching for an idea (or even lying in a hammock, as I discovered during the short-lived craze that accompanied a speculative purchase) may work for some, but not for me.

Often several fragments of an idea stay latent in my head for some time before they mature, gradually coming together to form something more coherent and reachable. Once cultivated, the idea is rarely in the form of a short story, or a poem, or even a series of pictures. The best way to describe it is like the idea for a film. The 'book' is played out in my head in a series of frames and scenes, and there is no divide between the words and the pictures; the two components are for ever inseparable. Throughout the formation of the idea my mind operates in much the same way as a film director. When children ask me how I make a picture book, I often tell them to imagine they have been lent a video camera and asked to film a day in their life. They *could* shoot every moment for an entire twenty-four hours. The film would cover every banal detail of their existence during this period: every meal; every routine; every bodily requirement; every social exchange; not to mention eight hours of sleep. It would be interminable for everybody, except perhaps the most ardent of *Big Brother* fans. What a film director does is reduce this material into a reasonable length, keeping the highlights and discarding the dross.

To do this the filmmaker creates a storyboard: a series of rectangles, each containing a rough drawing which represents a frame in the film. Its purpose is to provide a visual map of the entire movie at a very early stage of production. It is simply the first and most basic way for the director to express his idea. I do exactly the same thing when I plan a picture book. I draw out a series of twenty-four rectangles (representing the twelve double-page spreads which form the main part of a typical picture book), and fill them with very rough drawings and scrawls of text. In my case the rectangles represent the pages in the book, but I'm still thinking in filmic terms at this stage. In my mind there is a kind of animation to the idea, and I view my storyboard almost exactly as a filmmaker would. Rather than the fixed pictures they will eventually become, I view the boxes as frames or scenes from the story, with a clear sense of progression through time.

Using this method, the pictures and the words are devised together. The relationship in a film between the visual images and the verbal dialogue is crucial to its success, and I consider this relationship to be of equal importance in a picture book. 'Playing out' the book in this way ensures that the visual and the textual come to me at the same time. Although both are sketchily laid down in the story-board and will be changed before the final publication, it is important that they are laid down together, and remain a combinative force throughout the creative process.

Having made my storyboard, I make a photocopy (usually blowing the images up in order to counter their tiny scale), cut out the individual 'frames' and stick them into a small book. The result is a dummy: a mini version of a complete thirty-two-page picture book, endpapers included.

The dummy is the first incarnation of the idea that I show to my editor. With the dummy as a reference, we discuss the general qualities of the prospective book. There is rarely criticism of the pictures at this stage, but suggestions are offered as to how I could improve the text, the layout and the general rhythm.

I go back to my studio and set to work on the final pictures. I start by making slightly more detailed preliminary drawings on thin layout paper, the proportions of which correspond with the final book. As they are drawings, I can afford to make mistakes at this point, and with the aid of my putty rubber I alter as many details as I need to until I am satisfied with the image. One thing that is notable about the drawings at this stage is the absence of many details. If the illustration is of a woman and a boy walking in the park, that is all I will represent in the drawing, and any additional embellishments will be saved for the next, more improvisatory stage. This maintains my creative interest throughout the production of the final artwork. To make the final paintings just slicker versions of the preliminary drawings would dampen my interest, so I always leave plenty to create.

I transfer the drawings onto watercolour paper with graphite paper, using a very sharp, hard pencil to trace the image onto the new surface.

I like to soak the watercolour paper and stretch it on a board before painting. The main purpose of this is to flatten the surface so that it doesn't warp or bubble, and the paint is distributed evenly, but it also gives the paper a very special, precious quality.

The stretching process turns it into a smooth, flat, taut surface to work on, which not only makes the conditions perfect for painting but also puts me in the right state of mind. The beautifully prepared surface with its pristine whiteness gives the whole process an almost spiritual feel.

Many more traditional watercolour artists use roughly textured paper, which is conducive to the washy effect commonly associated with the medium, but I usually use smooth watercolour paper in order to achieve finer detail. I started to use

watercolour when I was a medical illustrator, and the demands of the job required me to be unusually attentive to detail. I admire the flowing style of traditional watercolourists, but the tight style that I adopted during my years at the hospital seems to suit my books, and I have generally tended to stick with it ever since.

It is very important that I have maximum access to daylight when I work. For years I worked in a purpose-built studio in my garden. Although I made sure there were plenty of windows, the profusion of trees in the garden – as well as the light-reducing effect of the crater in which the house stands (it is built on the grounds of an ancient chalk pit) – meant that it was never quite the heavenly environment in which I had imagined 'the artist' at work. A few years ago I moved into a brand-new house. The kitchen extends into a conservatory-like area, which is dominated by glass:

Chapter opener: *The Shape Game*, Doubleday. 2003

Opposite and below: roughs for *Into the Forest*, Walker Books, 2004

Above: my studio, 2010

as well as the windows, the door that leads to the garden is glass-paned, as is the roof. This part of the house seems to be bathed in light even on the darkest days. It is an ideal place to work.

One of the great things about the job is that I work from home; the conditions are on my terms. But although I can work whenever I like, I tend to operate fairly typical office hours, starting the day at about half past nine in the morning and working right through until it is time to prepare dinner in the evening. It is important for me to have this routine. I find it enjoyable and effective, and on the few occasions I have been forced to stray from it I have hated the lack of direction. Every now and then I will finish a project before I have thought of the next one, and the period during which I am

waiting for a new idea is torturous. My biggest fear is that I will eventually run out of ideas completely. I think the one thing that could drive me mad is having nothing to do.

My basic work process has remained fairly consistent throughout most of my career. As I've got older, however, my approach to each book has become more varied. Like an established pop group that – either in an effort to sustain critical appeal or to rekindle creative impetus – starts to stray from their reliable formula (perhaps by recruiting a didgeridoo), I have employed increasingly different strategies in recent years.

The start of this new outlook was embodied in *Voices in the Park*, for it is the first and only time I have revisited a previous book.

Although I grew to like the story, I was never happy with the illustrations in *A Walk in the Park*. I was very new to picture books when I made it and didn't really know what I was doing. Later I saw that the pictures were rushed and carelessly executed, and the background details were purely arbitrary, with little or no relevance to the story. Since *Hansel and Gretel*, I had learned to make the background 'incidentals' more significant. I employed them more shrewdly, as a way of commenting on the events in the foreground or revealing narrative secrets that were otherwise concealed.

The story deserved a better visual complement, and I knew that the illustrations would be far better if I were to do them now. But to simply repaint the pictures would be pointless and petty: a vain exercise hoping to show how much I had improved since the early days. I knew there was more I could develop from the story – that it left more to be said, but I wasn't sure what it was or how I was to say it. I eventually solved the problem by combining the *A Walk in the Park* re-work with another idea. Nearly all my books until this point had been written in the third person, and for some time I had wanted to create a book that told the same story from the perspectives of two or more first-person narrators. I wanted to show how the same event could be interpreted differently by different characters. The ability to empathize is a crucial life skill that it is important for all children to learn, and this was one of my reasons for creating *Voices in the Park*.

The book is based on exactly the same story as its twenty-year-old predecessor. Whereas *A Walk in the Park* was told from the point of view of a nameless narrator, however, *Voices in the Park* is a collection of four stories, told by the four main characters in the book. Although the stories all describe the same walk in the park, they contrast considerably, because each of the individuals interprets the event differently.

I mentioned before that it was this book that cast me into a period of mild depression, leading me to doubt my future in picture books. I was halfway through, and was bogged down with a painting of a dark winter scene. This, together with concerns about the relevancy of my style in the current picture-book climate, caused me to give up entirely for a period, before *Willy the Dreamer* provided the

necessary stimulus to nudge me out of the doldrums. Willy revived my enthusiasm for picture books completely.

I took the incomplete *Voices in the Park* back to my publisher, who vehemently urged for its completion, prompting me to return to the book with renewed verve. But for all my enthusiasm, I still couldn't get past the winter picture. I was no longer depressed, but some dissatisfaction with the book was preventing me from progressing. I studied the pictures I had made so far, and noticed that there was something wrong with the people. They were more or less the same characters that had appeared in *A Walk in the Park*, but, whereas in that book the summoning of visual clichés seemed like an effective way of evoking a playful sense of satire, in the context of *Voices in the Park* the stereotypes were somehow harder to swallow. I had to change them.

At that time, after finishing a painting, I would cover it with acetate for protection. I took one of the illustrations of Mrs Smythe and began altering her face by painting in gouache directly onto the acetate shield. I had no plan other than to make her look more 'real'; to make her a believable person as opposed to a crude stereotype. But as I played the Shape Game with her face, it was as if the movements of the paintbrush were beyond my control. I watched, infuriated, as my compulsion to turn her into a gorilla exerted itself. How typical! Was I really becoming such a parody of myself? The book wasn't supposed to be about gorillas; it was about people . . . real people.

But when I looked harder I saw that, miraculously, the problem was solved. The gorilla character lifted the book. The social stereotype vanished and the book became lighter, funnier, stranger and, in an unlikely way, more real. Once again, the universal quality of gorillas, their simultaneous representation of everybody and nobody, removed the specific categorization that readers ascribe to human characters.

I painted over the other characters' faces on the acetate, changing them all into gorillas. The result was pleasing and I was convinced that the gorillas improved the book immeasurably, but I was worried about showing my editor the drastic changes I had made to a book she was already pleased with. It would seem as if I was making fun of myself. If there was a comedy sketch show about children's book illustrators (an absurd concept, of course!), the weekly lampooning of Anthony Browne would probably feature the ape-obsessed buffoon butchering a series of increasingly serious texts by turning the main characters into gorillas. 'Hello, Mr Publisher? I've been working on this great new version of *The Odyssey*. You'll never guess what I've done!'

I went to see my editor, Penny Walker, with this concern, having told her nothing except that I had changed 'something' about the pictures. I knew I would be able to gauge her opinion as soon as she opened the book. She reacted very well, and agreed that it lifted the book to a new level. It was an immense relief that I had her support. I returned home, removed the acetate and painted over the human faces with gouache until they were all apes,

Above and opposite: *Voices in the Park*, Doubleday, 1998

but deliberately left the hands human. I wanted to make the point that although the characters are portrayed as gorillas, the book is still very much a study of human behaviour.

The main challenge for me was to make the four 'voices' look and sound as different as possible. This was fairly easy to do with the text. The posh Mrs Smythe's style is prim and sensible, and although her grammar is impeccable, her style shows neither embellishment nor imagination. The language that she uses betrays her bourgeois outlook. She describes the Smiths' dog as 'the horrible thing' and muses on the 'frightful types [that one sees] in the park these days!' The typeface of the text is in the neat, formal style of the broadsheet newspapers that she probably reads.

The illustrations allowed me to vary the ways in which I represented the voices. One way to illustrate the characters' circumstances was to employ the pathetic fallacy, so each narrator recalls the events taking place at a different time of year. Mrs Smythe's story is played out against the rich backdrop of autumn – the reds, yellows and golds representing her wealth and security.

The seasonal colours are just one way in which the style of illustration differs for each voice. The correctness of Mrs Smythe's narrative style is coupled with a detailed, realistic watercolour technique: seldom is a blade of grass neglected; never is the pattern of the wood grain on the park bench ignored.

The background details are also integral to the individual voices. As Mrs Smythe searches for her son, the trees behind her act as a kind of Greek chorus, looking on with open mouths, mocking the anger of her countenance.

As she lets Victoria off the lead, two distantly visible figures are about to cross paths: a beggar and a queen. This reinforces the reason – also evident in the main narrative – that I chose to set the story in a park. The park is not confined to a particular social class: all kinds of people walk their dogs there.

I mentioned before that I like to leave the hidden

details out of the pictures during the transfer process, preferring to improvise when I start to paint. I began painting the final picture of the Mrs Smythe sequence with this mindset, knowing that I would create something unanticipated in the process. For this illustration, I basked in the satisfying goldenness of the autumnal colours, making things glow wherever I could. Everything in the picture is imbued with an orange blush: the dog's leonine coat, the path that the characters have recently trod, the top of the lamppost, the windows of the buildings in the background and the leaves on the trees. My original intention was purely to evoke the spirit of autumn, but there was something else that influenced my treatment of the trees. The vividness of the orange made it seem as if they were burning and, at the time, this was what influenced my decision to paint one of the trees actually ablaze. But when I look back at the picture I think Mrs Smythe's mood also affected the decision. She herself is burning with anger as she marshals her miscreant son home.

I deliberately painted Charles so that he is barely visible, engulfed by his domineering mother. I think I have a tendency to empathize with the characters I paint, and quite often their feelings are reflected in surprising parts of the illustration. It is a process that seems to be beyond my control.

All the voices are supplemented by visual clues which reveal their states of mind. Whereas Mrs Smythe was first shown leaving her large, majestic house, I have deliberately introduced Mr Smith

against a plain white background. We don't see where he lives at all: his armchair appears to be floating in limbo.

On the opposite page is the illustration that I struggled to complete. Mr Smith's depression is amplified by the winter season. The bare trees droop forlornly, echoing the curve of the narrator's hunched back; the famously cheery expressions of the Laughing Cavalier and the Mona Lisa are dramatically down-turned in the reproductions that adorn the pavement, surrounded by a pool of tears; and such is the hellish quality of the sky that one expects to see the outstretched arms of tortured souls thrusting from the windows of the tower

blocks, which, hideous though they are, do little to blot what is already a wretched landscape. The two main characters and their dog are about to pass the jolliest man on earth, but in Mr Smith's bleak portrait Father Christmas has been reduced to a miserable street beggar.

By the time Mr Smith returns from the park, however, his spirits have lifted. The happy chatting of his daughter has reminded him of the special relationship that they share, and he realizes that no matter how dire his circumstances, they cannot extinguish the warm, loving light that she shines on his life. Consequently, when they reach the same point on the return journey, the scene has changed. Again, I have referenced the spot-the-difference puzzles that I loved as a child: the previous details survive, but they have all been altered to reflect Mr Smith's renewed optimism. Father Christmas is still there, but instead of begging he is performing a ballet routine, while the Laughing Cavalier and the Mona Lisa express their appreciation of the silent music by dancing a passionate tango. The trees have corrected their posture and stand erect, baring the celestial fruit of the night sky. The lamppost has bloomed into a flower, but the golden light that spotlights Smudge and her father emanates not from its snowdrop bulb but from Smudge herself, her buoyant personality brightening the whole scene. Kong flexes his muscles triumphantly atop one of the tower blocks in the background, the

Opposite and right: *Voices in the Park*, Doubleday, 1998

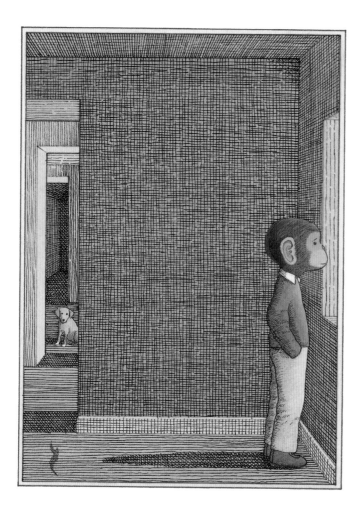

Trapped in his room; trapped in his life; trapped in the book. The background reveals a series of doorways: a purgatorial network of rooms within rooms within rooms, with no obvious exit to the outside world.

When they arrive at the park, the naked trees suggest a winter setting, just like Mr Smith's narration, but the bleakness is perhaps even more pronounced in Charles's world, infused as it is with a sense of hopeless rigidity which is evident in every aspect. Even the trees have grown into obsessively perfect shapes: not a twig is out of place.

We view Charles from behind, and the dark, ominous shape that seems to root his feet to the ground confirms that he walks literally in his mother's shadow. The precise shape of her trilby corresponds with the overall neatness of the illustrations, but, in the context of Charles's oppression, it also has vague military connotations. Her dictatorship is confirmed by the repetition of the hat motif in virtually every object that Charles can see. The typeface is an austere, spidery font, reminiscent of that associated with a typewriter.

Once Charles meets Smudge, however, things begin to change. Although their parents have determined that they sit at opposite ends of the bench, Smudge breaks the shackles by initiating contact with Charles, inviting him to play on the slide. For this illustration I have tried to show the appeal of Smudge and her free, fun-seeking lifestyle, which Charles longs to be involved in. A black lamppost divides the two children spatially, representing a

windows of which are lit up with an array of bright colours. Some of them are in the shapes of hearts and stars.

The third voice is that of Charles – Mrs Smythe's overprotected son. The style of illustration is immediately distinctive. Although the pictures are painted in watercolour washes, the colours are flat and grey, and the detail is rendered in pen and ink. Charles is denied the child's need to flourish and play, and the tight cross-hatching style of the drawings emphasizes his feelings of entrapment.

In the first image, he is trapped in every sense.

Opposite and above:
Voices in the Park, Doubleday, 1998

clear boundary for the tempted Charles. On his side of the lamppost the gloom persists. The dark clouds gather on the horizon, the cross-hatching and individually defined blades of grass continue to lock him into the illustration, and the dark trees make for a charmless backdrop. But on Smudge's side spring has already arrived, indicated by the paler green of the grass, the blossom on the trees and the clear blue sky. On her horizon the clouds abruptly clear, to reveal a castle: a castle that is, in her fairy-tale world, as enchanted as she wishes it to be.

In the background of the illustration, two figures (a man and a woman) appear to be cycling past each other on the hill. But look closely and you will see that they are in fact riding the same bike, pedalling in opposite directions. Perhaps the woman represents Smudge, attempting to tug Charles up the hill towards the brightness?

Mercifully, Charles accepts Smudge's invitation, and gradually his world becomes a better place. The clouds part, and while spring begins to take hold, the fading and ultimate evaporation of the hat motif from the illustrations implies that Charles's mother is, for now at least, losing her grip on the boy's freedom.

Charles has a wonderful time with Smudge. Although the reflection in the metal of the slide betrays his terror, Charles revels in the new experience. I have tried to suggest the speed and drama of his imminent descent by painting the slide extending over the edge of the frame, so that it is possible to imagine Charles whooshing right off the page: perhaps his exit to ultimate freedom

beyond the confines of the book itself . . .

Despite the fact that 'Mummy [catches them] talking together' and Charles has to go home, his new feelings of hope prevail on the final page. 'Maybe Smudge will be there next time?' he muses, her influence clinging to him in the form of a trail of blossom at his heels. The cross-hatching is abandoned in favour of a smoother, looser water-colour style. The colours are dominated by the radiant orange glow of the early evening sunset – a far cry from the depressing greys and blues which saturated the early part of the story.

Smudge provides the fourth voice. Predictably, it is summer. The colours are bright and flamboyant. The style is cartoonish and the world that she inhabits is a veritable wonderland, full of joy. She plays the Shape Game with everything she sees. As they enter the park, the lamppost is adorned with a royal crown, and there is a giant strawberry amongst the trees. When she looks across at Charles and his mother on the bench, the trees in the background are an assortment of fruits, and the statues on the fountain are gorillas, each sporting a different (but equally enviable) pair of swimming shorts.

The final picture is a resurrection of that in *A Walk in the Park*, but it carries a great deal more significance. In the original version of the story, Charles picks a flower and gives it to Smudge. The final page has no text – just the simple image of the flower in a jam jar on the windowsill. Smudge has kept it. On the final page of *Voices in the Park*, she tells us that she has 'put the flower in some water',

and the illustration verifies this, but whereas the flower was nondescript in the first book, this time it is evidently a poppy. It isn't just a flower: it is a symbol of remembrance. It isn't a jam jar either: it is a mug, and the childish design depicts a park scene with two very familiar dogs.

I have always loved to play with shadows and reflections. Shadows are an expedient way of showing a hidden side to a character. They can also be used to depict a character's true feelings, underneath the external façade. I love J. M. Barrie's concept of the shadow being a separate entity to its owner, with a cultivated quality of independence. It may be an obvious statement, but the beauty of fiction is that it isn't real. In books, there is no reason why a shadow cannot contradict the physical nature of the object that casts it.

In the final picture for *Voices in the Park*, the shadow of the flower on the wall is a similar shape to the flower itself, but it also resembles a speech bubble. I am tempted – as I have been at several points when describing examples of the Shape Game in my books – to use the common term 'visual metaphor' to describe my treatment of the

Opposite and above: *Voices in the Park*, Doubleday, 1998

shadow. But that would imply the wrong message. I am not saying that the flower is a speech bubble; rather that it is like a speech bubble, or that it can be like a speech bubble if the reader chooses it to be. It may not be in common circulation, but a more accurate term would be 'visual simile', and this is how I shall refer to such images from now on.

In this case, the flower/speech bubble visual simile implies that there is an additional unheard voice; perhaps even several, or infinite, unheard voices. Nobody has ever told me that they have drawn this conclusion from the speech-bubble shadow, but many children have written extra voices for the story – the most popular choice being one of the dogs. I like to think that the final picture encourages the reader to wonder about the potential for further narrators.

Voices in the Park was a very different kind of book from all its predecessors, but at least it was entirely my own conception. By 2001 I had written and illustrated nearly thirty books, and although I had been in positions where I had relinquished a certain amount of control (I had illustrated a number of books by other authors), I had never been obliged to produce a book under specific conditions.

In the early part of the year I was approached by Colin Grigg from Tate Britain. Colin was the co-ordinator of a project called Visual Paths, which was developed by the Tate in partnership with the Institute of Education. He asked if I would be interested in being the artist in residence at the gallery from June 2001 until March 2002. He

Above: *Voices in the Park*, Doubleday, 1998

proposed that I work with a thousand children from inner-city schools, teaching them literacy in the context of the gallery. I would direct a series of workshops, during which the children would respond to the works of art. At the end of my term at the gallery, it was intended that I create a picture book, inspired by the experience.

I was incredibly flattered to be asked. I love Tate Britain. It sounded like a fantastic scheme, which would allow me to complement the attempts in my books to get children to appreciate fine art. In my immediate elation I gladly accepted Colin's offer, and it was only later, when I had digested everything he had said, that the pressure descended. The workshops would no doubt be enjoyable, but the idea of having to come up with an idea based on the events was a nightmare for someone with my capacity for worry. As much as I love visiting art galleries, the subject doesn't exactly scream for the picture-book treatment, and I began to anticipate months of sleepless nights, hopelessly groping for ideas. Ideas only ever come to me organically, and never when I search for them. This enforced process seemed horribly alien to me.

Moreover, I felt that I had already made the book they were asking for. *Willy the Dreamer* and, to an even greater extent, *Willy's Pictures* are specifically about looking at paintings. The latter is probably the book I would have created for the Tate project, had it not existed already. Its premise is essentially a tour through Willy's personal art gallery, teaching children about great paintings and how to make them 'come alive'. It would have fitted the scheme perfectly. But it was useless to dwell on this. I had committed myself to the project and had to come up with a new idea.

Before I began working at the gallery I was to meet some teachers in London to talk about the project. I was supposed to explain to them how the workshops would operate and how the teachers would contribute. This would enable them to prepare their children for the workshops in class before they came to the gallery.

But when I got on the train to London in the morning I still hadn't a clue what the final book would be about. Consequently, I hadn't thought much about the workshops because their content was supposed to relate to the book. I had nothing to say to them!

I had rushed to get ready that morning, with no time to open the post, so I took it with me on the train. From time to time my publishers send me reviews and articles about my books, and among the letters on this particular morning was an article about the book, Zoo. It was tremendously serendipitous, because had my mind not been preoccupied with the talk later that day I might not have made the connection. It suddenly made total sense to revisit the family from Zoo, this time on a trip to Tate Britain.

I thought about it for the duration of the train journey. Having woken up that morning (from the little sleep I'd had) with no idea what I would say to the teachers, by the time I arrived in London I had formulated a passable plan for both the book and the relating workshops.

If the new book was to be about the family from Zoo, it would help if the children were well versed in the original text before they came to the workshops, so I encouraged the teachers to work with the children on Zoo – reading and discussing it with them, studying the pictures and, above all, getting to know the individual characters. I wanted the children to expand their knowledge of the family beyond what is revealed in the story: what would they say is Dad's favourite television programme? What is Harry's favourite subject at school?

For the next few weeks, before the workshops started, I spent a lot of time in the Tate, looking at the pictures. There were hundreds of paintings and I needed to work out a specific angle that would encompass only a few of them.

As I looked at the more illustrative paintings, I noticed a common feature that was very familiar. Many of the paintings contain hidden clues that reveal more about the story behind the painting than the main visual subject does on its own.

This is exactly what I try to do in my books. Great painters use symbols of brilliant subtlety: references to mythology, history and culture that provide additional information about the story. I listened to the educators at the Tate talk about the masterpieces to groups of viewers, and it was amazing how much they were able to make the paintings 'open up' by educating us in their numerous subtleties.

I continued to work closely with Colin Grigg throughout the project. He was a superb co-ordinator, with a passion for art. His job was to enlighten children and teachers, providing them with ideas for class projects that focused on the works in the gallery. The philosophy of Visual Paths was that 'works of art provide a unique stimulus for creative writing and language development . . . Engaging with rich imagery of works of art can form a powerful bridge in coming to terms with a new culture and language.' The main reason I was so willing to participate in the project was that I shared this philosophy entirely.

One of the most enduring things Colin told me was that he compared himself to a zookeeper. By opening up the paintings, he felt as if he was opening up the cages in a zoo, allowing children to engage with the exotic 'captives'. The analogy appealed to me. Zoos and animals have always been a source of fascination, and hearing Colin compare the paintings to living, breathing creatures was like hearing somebody voice my dream of bringing art to life. He believed in children and art as much as I did, and it was exciting to find somebody who worked with similar motives.

I chose several paintings that I could imagine the family from Zoo engaging with. I have looked at countless paintings in galleries, but never with this approach, and it was interesting to survey the gallery in the context of the story, imagining what each of the family members would say about the paintings. I thought that the children might enjoy a similar exercise, so when they came to the gallery I divided them into four groups: one group was Dad; one group was Mum; one was the older boy; and one the younger boy. It was a bit like a drama exercise. Experience taught me that it was best to limit the children's range to one room of the gallery. I asked them to look at the paintings in character, reacting to what they saw as they imagined their particular family member would, to the very last detail. For example, I encouraged those in the Dad group to walk like Dad as they went from painting to painting; to say the things he would say; to feel the way he would feel; to scratch themselves the way he would scratch himself!

I also got them to imagine themselves or their characters in the paintings. Where would George fit in here? Why would he be there? How could the painting be changed in order to accommodate him?

Afterwards I got the children to make drawings based on their thoughts. They made copies of the pictures, with themselves or the characters from *Zoo* included somehow. Underneath the drawing, they wrote a caption. It might be a short sentence to describe what was going on in the picture; it might be a comment from one of the characters, or a suggestion of their thoughts. I gave them plenty of freedom.

Finally I took the children back to the studio in the museum and talked to them about pictures, focusing on how seemingly inessential details can help to tell the whole story. I showed them two of my illustrations from *Zoo* as examples: the picture of the father, viewed from below, with the horn-like formation of the clouds indicating his inner wrath; and the image of the tiger pacing up and down the cage – the repetition of its movements represented by the grass, which grows to form the tiger's mirrored image walking in the opposite direction. I compared my techniques with a painting from the gallery called 'Past and Present, No. 1' by Augustus Egg – a painting in which virtually every detail contributes to the story behind the scene.

All I explained to the children was the picture's basic content. It is a Victorian family scene. The father/husband has discovered a letter to his wife from another man, and the painting illustrates the immediate aftermath. I told the children that there are several clues in the painting which reveal more about what is happening. Together we pieced

Above: *Past and Present, No.1*, Augustus Egg. 1858

together the puzzle.

On the wall on the left-hand side of the mirror is a painting of Adam and Eve. The biblical couple were cast out of Paradise after Eve was tempted to eat the serpent's apple. It would seem that the crumpled woman in the foreground of Egg's painting has also succumbed to temptation from another man, a portrait of whom lies crushed beside her husband's foot.

On the other side of the mirror is a painting of a broken ship, abandoned by its crew: a clear metaphor for the cuckolded husband, who also feels abandoned.

In the mirror we can see the reflection of an open door. This foreshadows the woman's imminent departure from the house and from the family; perhaps even from society.

The children are occupied with their house of

cards, but their painstaking construction is falling down, reflecting the disintegration of their actual home life.

The woman has fallen to the floor, her hands clasped together in anguish, and the bracelets on her wrists are painted to look like handcuffs. In the context of Victorian England, it is a heinous crime she has committed. On the floor beside her is one half of an apple, which is rapidly decaying: the 'bad half'. As well as being another reference from Genesis (the forbidden fruit), it also represents the decay of the nuclear family, and we are encouraged to associate its state of decomposition with the 'rotten' nature of the woman's conduct.

The 'good half' remains on the table. It is painted somewhat ambiguously, bearing a resemblance – sufficient enough for the purposes of symbolism – to the heart of the nearby husband. Appropriately enough, it is skewered by a knife.

I talked to the children about the symbols, and in every case it was they, not I, who interpreted them. As we analysed the complicated scene, which dealt with such adult themes as adultery, heartbreak and betrayal, I was concerned it would be over their heads, but, as has happened so often throughout my career, the children surprised and delighted me with their ability to understand very difficult concepts. Many people are tempted to condescend to children even though, with visual material in particular, they are usually far more perceptive than we give them credit for.

The children returned to their schools and continued to work on projects based on their experience at the gallery. Meanwhile, I tried to develop a story about the Zoo family visiting Tate Britain. The book that I produced was inspired by the Visual Paths project in many ways, some more obvious than others. One of the less obvious parallels was the relationship between my feelings as I underwent the project and those of the Zoo family as they wander through the gallery. I too felt outside my natural environment in the context of the museum. Although I had talked to groups of children many times in the past and was familiar with art galleries as an ordinary member of the public, I had never worked in a gallery, and had certainly never been in the position of having to create a book based on a specific experience.

I also felt uncomfortable because it was a difficult environment in which to work. Trying to keep the attention of twenty children in an enormous public room, with people constantly walking past, was very challenging, and the children themselves were uncomfortable because most of them had never been to a gallery before. Naturally they were quiet and shy for much of the sessions, trying to come to terms with the strangeness of the place. But the difficulties I went through in order to create the book ironically helped me to shape it. I used my feelings of discomfort and transposed them into the context of the protagonists as they tried to cope with the museum environment themselves. They are hardly the most cultured of families, and, like the children I had been working with, this was probably their

first time in an art gallery (the mother excepted). I imagined they would feel similarly lost as they walked through the vast, intimidating rooms, the portraits glaring at them from all angles.

I tried to convey these feelings in the first part of the book, which I called *The Shape Game*. The book opens with the image of an artist, painting in his studio. It isn't an autobiographical story (the model is in fact my brother, Michael), but the character is (as I was when I made the illustration) a children's book illustrator, working on a book. The text reads, 'I was a little boy and didn't know what to expect. It was my mother's idea – that year for her birthday she wanted us all to go somewhere different. It turned out to be a day that changed my life for ever.'

From this point on, it is clear that the rest of the book is a flashback. The artist (who turns out to be the younger boy, Harry) proceeds to recall 'that special day'.

'Somewhere different' turns out to be Tate Britain. The first few illustrations are painted in shades of sepia, reflecting the lack of enthusiasm among the males as they resign themselves to a

Above: *The Shape Game*, Doubleday, 2003

Above and opposite:
The Shape Game, Doubleday, 2003

boring day at the museum. They would rather watch the 'important match on the telly'. As they walk alongside the Thames, the only splash of colour is the blue of the river – a reminder that the story is being told in retrospect by the grown-up Harry, for whom hindsight has paved the road with yellow bricks. Its destination is far more Oz-like to him now than it seemed in prospect.

The illustration shows the museum in all its glory. I painted it viewed from below (the family yet to ascend the steps that lead to the entrance) and I like to think that this view helps to convey the daunting impression of the building. The image appears naturalistic, but look closely at the details of the building and you will see that I have played the

Shape Game extensively.

Though undeniably splendid, the Tate seems to the boys like an overgrown mass of cold, inhospitable stone. As with the river, a ray of hope is offered by the mysterious turquoise that shines from the windows.

They enter the museum. The characters remain in sepia, while the inside of the museum is an icy blue. They are a little nervous. Dad's comments about the paintings are as ignorant and puerile as they were about the animals at the zoo.

'What's that supposed to be?' he asks about an abstract sculpture.

'It's supposed to be a mother and child,' replies his wife.

'Well, why isn't it?'
One by one, however, the characters begin to engage with the paintings. Mum – always a frustrated aesthete – is the first to come around. Gradually, as her appreciation of the artwork revives her spirits, more and more colour enters her appearance, until eventually her cardigan is a striking scarlet. For the illustration which accompanies her leading the family into 'a large room that was full of old paint-ings' I have played with the design a little. The illustration is enclosed within a border resembling a picture frame. It is as if we, the viewers, are in a gallery ourselves, looking at a painting of the family looking at paintings. George's assessment of the room as 'boring' is shared by his father and, to a lesser extent, his brother. Consequently the three males are on the same plane as the viewer. They are suppos-

edly inside the room, but they observe the scene from outside the frame, as does the reader; the border of the illustration fails to contain them. They see the room and the paintings within, but they are not yet in the picture. Mum, on the other hand, is painted on the inside of the frame because she has, in a sense, got 'inside' the artwork.

Gradually, as they proceed through the gallery, every member of the family finds at least one painting to appreciate. Their feelings of alienation subside and they begin to enjoy themselves. As the paintings come to life, their appearances change, until they are all painted in bright colours – colours they have seemingly inherited from the beautiful art around them.

The Shape Game is partly an attempt to help children understand the joy of art, but although it was born out of the schools sessions, which were supervised by teachers and part of the curriculum, I was determined that the book should not be overly educational. I infused it wherever I could with jokes and puzzles. Once again I resurrected the spot-the-difference puzzles that I had used so often in the past, and it became a recurring theme to juxtapose the original paintings with alternative versions, imagined by the family, often involving Dad indulging in various acts of buffoonery.

In this way I was able to maintain the formula

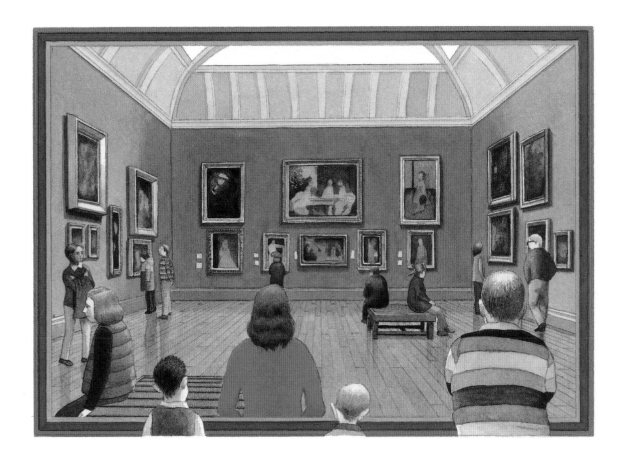

of *Zoo* to some extent. The original paintings are the equivalent of the animals in the first book: serious, real, poignant. Alongside the paintings are the family's behavioural responses: just as fatuous as before, only this time more imaginative and benign. At first, the male characters are as scornful of the artwork as they were of the animals, but the scorn soon dissolves when they learn to use their imaginations. In contrast to the trip to the zoo, the Tate visit is an unlikely success for everybody.

The idea to bring the Shape Game into the book came quite late on. I played the game constantly as I illustrated *The Shape Game* – with both the reinterpretations of the original paintings and the details in the background. It was also very much on my mind at the time because I had recently started teaching it to children in schools and bookshops. This is how I learned that all children

love the Shape Game, and that many have already discovered it for themselves before I 'introduce' it to them. But it struck me that I had played the Shape Game for so long without ever bringing it to the foreground of my books. It seemed like the perfect ending to my current book for Mum to teach her boys – and, ultimately, all boys and girls who read the book – how to play the Shape Game. On the train journey home, she does exactly that. The last double-page spread and endpapers show the results of the family's Shape Game.

The examples that are displayed are in fact the products of many Shape Games I have played with children.

The Visual Paths project was difficult at times and I was forced to work outside my comfort zone. Ultimately, however, it was a fantastic experience. I had been making picture books for years, working entirely on my own terms the whole time. All the books I had produced before had presented their own set of challenges, but usually all it took to overcome them was a little patience. On the few occasions that patience hadn't been enough, I always knew that I could abandon the book and come back to it later if I chose. In the case of *The Shape Game*, I was obliged to produce a book, working under someone else's scheme. Daunting though the prospect was, I am pleased with the outcome and I look back on the Visual Paths project as a very enjoyable and worthwhile period in my career.

Opposite, left: *The Meeting* or
Have a Nice Day, Mr Hockney,
Peter Blake, 1981-1983
Above and opposite, right:
The Shape Game, Doubleday, 2003

Chapter Ten

Working With Writers

write the vast majority of my books myself, but I have illustrated a number of texts by other authors. This is a quite different experience. In some ways it is harder, for the pictures rarely come to mind as easily, but it can be useful, particularly when I am struggling for an idea of my own.

It is flattering when a writer (especially one whose work I have admired for a while) approaches me with a request to illustrate his or her work. The majority of the texts passed on to me by publishers are either unsuitable for my style or else fail to capture my imagination; these are the texts which are easy to turn down. But I read every text that comes my way, and occasionally my tolerance is rewarded when something creates a spark.

The first book by another author that I revelled in illustrating was *The Visitors Who Came to Stay* by Annalena McAfee. The partnership between Annalena's

words and my pictures worked very well in the end, but the book didn't leap to life immediately.

Annalena was a close friend I had known for a long time. I knew that she was an excellent writer, but when she first showed me the story, I couldn't see much to grab hold of from an illustrator's perspective. Poignant and well written, it was about a girl whose tranquil life with her father is turned upside down when he gets a flamboyant new girlfriend. As if this wasn't enough for the sensitive Katy, a mischievous prankster son is also part of the package.

I enjoyed reading the story very much, but, as is often the case when I am presented with someone else's text, I found it hard to imagine my illustrations alongside it. The film that usually plays out in my head when I form my own ideas could gather no momentum with Annalena's story. A few images flitted in and out of my mind, but they were nebulous at best, and there was a constant disparity between the words and the pictures.

I wanted to illustrate *The Visitors Who Came to Stay* because I liked Annalena, I liked the story and I liked the idea of working with somebody else after working alone for so long, but I couldn't find a way in. The problem was that not a lot actually *happened* in the story. It was more about feelings than events. How do you illustrate a book about feelings?

I talked about the problem with Annalena, and she suggested that one way of solving it might be to have a theme running through. We both had houses near the sea, so we wondered about the seaside as a theme we might explore. It sounded like a viable suggestion at first, but further discussion led us to realize that its suitability was perfect: a brilliant parallel for the events of the story lay in the unique nature of the British seaside. Just as Katy's world is transformed from the peaceful place she inhabits with her father into the loud, gaudy place it becomes when the visitors arrive, the schizophrenic seaside transforms from its Dr Jekyll winter state – calm, pensive, dormant – into a relative Mr Hyde of summer frenzy.

The idea opened the book up for me, and suddenly the pictures started to come to mind. Using the two different 'personalities' of the seaside, I could reflect Katy's state of mind before and after the arrival of the visitors.

I had an excellent working relationship with Annalena. She got the balance between interjection and retreat perfectly. As the author, she knew the characters very well and had a fairly clear idea of how

Chapter opener: *The Daydreamer*, Jonathan Cape, 1994

Above and overleaf: *The Visitors Who Came to Stay*,
Hamish Hamilton Children's Books, 1984

she imagined them to look, but she was never tempted to dictate anything, and most of the decisions were made after discussing our ideas together. It was refreshing to have another mind to consult like this. During the development of the book we would have long conversations, discussing such details as what the father might wear at the breakfast table, and over time our separate internalizations of the characters became more and more similar.

Another thing that was helpful about Annalena's approach was that she was prepared to change the text as the pictures developed. Some authors write the text and expect to have nothing more to do with it until it is illustrated. The illustrator's job is simply to illustrate the finalized text and there is no question of the author adapting it to accommodate the illustrator's pictorial decisions. But Annalena viewed the creation of the book as a partnership. She was as open to my ideas as I was to hers, and if my pictures altered the course of the story slightly, she was happy to change the text accordingly. I was very much at ease, because she made the experience similar to that which I was used to. When I work autonomously, the words and the pictures are the same entity; they grow and mature together, constantly adapting to suit each whim and fancy. Annalena embraced this approach, which took a lot of pressure away.

The book came immediately after *Gorilla*, and I used many of the same strategies which had worked for that in *The Visitors Who Came to Stay*. *Gorilla* was the first time I had tactically emphasized the differences between the foreground events and the background

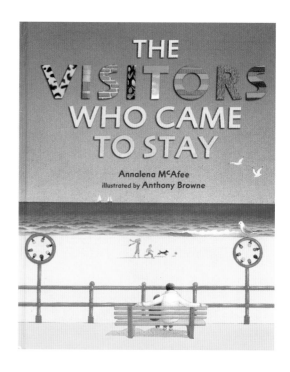

details. An author has the facility to describe in words what a character is thinking, but artists have to use more subtle devices. *The Visitors Who Came to Stay* is all about Katy's feelings, which she hides from the world for much of the story. I had originally been intimidated by the idea of illustrating a book about feelings, but I soon learned that it was the perfect vehicle for my developing style. As with *Gorilla*, I painted the protagonist behaving in a certain way, while the background details reveal what she is really feeling. This method, which has become synonymous with my work over the years, is perhaps at its most pronounced when I am illustrating someone else's texts. Because I have less control over the words, my tendency is to contribute as much to the story as I possibly can with the pictures. My only way of 'writing' the story is through the illustrations, and this is perhaps why the pictures are so riddled with narrative clues.

Since *The Visitors Who Came to Stay* I have illustrated a handful of texts by other authors. The most memorable of these was by a writer who, by sheer coincidence, became Annalena's husband: Ian McEwan.

Ian has always been one of my favourite writers. By the time he wrote his first children's book, *The Daydreamer*, I had read every book he had written, and I felt in a sense that I had grown up with his writing. He is a similar age to me, and started writing as a young man (often about the experience of *being* a young man), and without necessarily identifying with his every character, I certainly felt that he wrote about the world I knew. This affinity with his writing has continued as I have got older, and I still eagerly anticipate his every publication.

Back in 1994 I had already started to work on *King Kong* when I heard from somebody at Random House that they were publishing Ian McEwan's first children's book. Suspecting that the text would be brilliant and excited by the idea of working alongside one of my favourite writers, I did something I have never done before or since: I told Random House that I would be interested in illustrating McEwan's new book.

I am sometimes sent texts by other writers, but it's rare that I read something that really grabs me. *The Daydreamer* is the only book that I have actively pursued. The fact that I had not even read the text before wanting to work with it says a lot about my regard for Ian McEwan.

By the time I declared my interest to Random House they had already asked Maurice Sendak to take on the project, so I abandoned the idea and got back to work on *King Kong*. Not long after, however, the publishers phoned to tell me that Sendak would no longer be illustrating and to ask if I would like to do it after all. I was happy to, but the circumstances were hardly ideal. Random House wanted *The Daydreamer* to be ready by a certain date, and I was already heavily involved with *King Kong*, which also had a deadline. I had signed both contracts, and had no option but to work like a Trojan. I worked on *King Kong* during the day and *The Daydreamer* in the evening, the pensive black and white illustrations of the latter seeming more appropriate for the post-daylight hours.

It was the first time I had illustrated a book in black and white. Random House made the request in the interest of containing printing costs, but although the reasons were practical, they might just as well have been creative. Ian's diversion into children's writing maintained much of the dark, introspective qualities that are often associated with his adult fiction. I thought that the realistic black and white illustrations complemented *The Daydreamer* quite well.

Working in the evening helped to put me in the right frame of mind for the book, for under the unfamiliar twilight conditions and the effect of a day's slaving away at *King Kong* I was feeling a little dreamy myself. Creating the strange colourless paintings in my garden studio, surrounded by natural darkness, with nothing but artificial light for illumination, I felt isolated and a tiny bit afraid. These feelings were

appropriate in the context of the book.

When I met Ian for the first time, I brought the few illustrations I had made. He was vaguely familiar with my style and knew that the illustrations would be in black and white, but had little more idea of what to expect. He liked the pictures, but he seemed surprised at the particular moments in the text I had chosen to illustrate. I think a lot of writers imagine that the illustrations will capture the more dramatic, swashbuckling moments in the story. These are often the passages which are described with the most attention to detail, making them seem the most natural candidates for illustrative support. This is exactly why I tend to avoid illustrating them. It isn't required. The author has done all the work with the words. A picture, rather than complementing the

Above and opposite: *The Daydreamer*, Jonathan Cape, 1994

description, would simply undermine it, distracting the reader away from the author's intentions. For me, the illustrations are far more effective if they accompany the less obvious moments in the book, capturing the general sense of the story, evoking an atmosphere rather than dictating how the reader should visualize a certain incident. *The Daydreamer*, as the title would suggest, is quite an internal, contemplative book that deals with the protagonist's thoughts and feelings. I tried to enhance this aspect by making pictures that captured the spirit of the boy's daydreams, without painting the most descriptive moments within them.

It was perhaps most pronounced in *The Daydreamer*, but I always approach other authors' texts with this mindset. Every picture tells a story, but the artist has to take care when there are words involved, because the different stories can clash. Pictures can interfere with, as well as complement, the words. With my own books it is less of a concern, because they are my words and

I can treat them with as much regard or disdain as I like. With this knowledge, I can afford to indulge in the relationship between the words and the pictures, celebrating rather than fighting its fluctuant nature. Often the story of the illustration contradicts that of the words, but because both components are my own design, I can afford to take risks. With other people's texts, I am obliged to show more respect for the writing. It is important as an illustrator to know when to retreat and allow the words to speak for themselves.

The Daydreamer is one of a handful of longer texts I have illustrated. With *King Kong* I found my limit (I cannot see myself attempting a work of that intensity again), but I occasionally enjoy the different challenges that longer books present.

The first novel-length work I illustrated was *Alice's Adventures in Wonderland* in 1988. Julia MacRae had for a while been encouraging me to tackle a longer book. She thought I had reached a point in my career where I was established enough to illustrate a classic children's book, and the one that sprang immediately to her mind was *The Wizard of Oz*. I was keen on the idea at first, but I read the book and, as is so often the case, even with the best works of literature, I couldn't imagine my pictures alongside the text. If I am to develop an enthusiasm for illustrating another writer's story, I have to be able to visualize my illustrations. As much as I admire it, L. Frank Baum's story didn't cry out for the Anthony Browne treatment.

I discussed several other classics with Julia before I decided on *Alice*. I say 'I' as opposed to 'we', because it was purely my decision in the end, *Alice's Adventures in Wonderland* being one of the few 'great' children's books that Julia doesn't much care for. I, on the other hand, had always loved it, and it was my enthusiasm that brought Julia around to the idea.

As with *Hansel and Gretel* several years before, I was tentative about taking on the *Alice* project, because I knew that so many illustrators (over a hundred in fact) had illustrated it before me. Many had enjoyed great success but, of all the previous versions, the most persistent ghost (which must have haunted all but one of my predecessors) was the original edition, illustrated by Sir John Tenniel.

There are seminal recordings of certain songs which render the song virtually impossible to cover with any dignity thereafter. Chet Baker's 'My Funny Valentine'; Nina Simone's 'I Put a Spell on You'; anything by Randy Newman. It seems that they cannot be bettered. Tenniel's timeless line drawings, which complement Carroll's text so perfectly, are the illustrational equivalent of this.

For a while I wrestled with the problem of how to get past Tenniel's legacy, until I remembered that *Alice's Adventures in Wonderland* is about a dream. Dreams are unique to the dreamer, and just because Tenniel's drawings are so good doesn't mean that his 'interpretation of dreams' had to be the last word.

My Tenniel hang-up was further reduced when I read that the original drawings were not to Lewis Carroll's liking. So disappointed was he with Tenniel's job that when he had written the sequel, *Through the Looking-Glass*, he tried to find another illustrator, and eventually returned to Sir John only because he had failed to find somebody more suitable. The presumably wounded Tenniel proceeded to illustrate *Through the Looking-Glass* brilliantly, but found out that the only thing Carroll liked about the drawings was his rendering of Humpty Dumpty!

I was consoled, but I was still worried about the unspoken 'graduation' that the project represented. Most illustrators wait until they have attained a certain degree of eminence in the children's literature world before they dare to apply for a place 'on the board'. Julia thought I was ready; I wasn't so sure. But I came to realize that it was a silly hang-up. The text was ideal for me, and instead of becoming preoccupied with the superficialities associated with the more intimidating side of the book's culture, I told myself to put personal insecurities aside. It was just another book after all.

Nevertheless, the problem of 'getting around' Tenniel was forever at the back of my mind. My concerns led to the employment of various tactics,

intended to make my version as different as possible. For the illustration of the Mad Hatter, for example, instead of painting him to look mad in a wacky sense, I split his face down the middle. One half is arranged into a friendly smile; the other is dramatically down-turned in apparent misery. On the surface, and as far as my child readers are concerned, this just looks slightly peculiar, but on another level I was suggesting madness in a literal, psychiatric sense. It could be said that my Hatter is truly mad, his dual emotions schizophrenic.

Escaping the clutches of Tenniel's influence proved even harder when painting the Duchess. Tenniel's stunning caricature was inspired by an etching he had seen at the National Gallery. It has always been the grotesque, swollen product of Tenniel's pen that comes to mind whenever I think about the character. As with the Hatter, I needed a specific angle in order to get away from this preconception, so I decided to use the Duchess's baby as an inspiration. The baby turns into a pig, and I transposed the pig theme into the context of the Duchess's appearance, manipulating her features until they were undeniably erring on the porcine side. Her clothes are pink, the bow on her head is pink and ear-like, and her nose is upturned into a snout.

Needless to say, I didn't shy away from the surrealist aspects of the text. The book was reputedly favoured among the surrealists, which is hardly surprising, as it is packed with surrealist imagery. I decided not only to acknowledge the surrealist overtones, but to treat the project almost as an exercise in surrealist painting. As I illustrated *Alice's Adventures in Wonderland*, I tried to imagine how the likes of Magritte or Dali would have approached it; hence the proliferation of surrealist references in my version.

The text made it easy for me. Carroll's verbal puns are an irresistible vehicle for surrealist imagery. Creating these puns was a poetic game for him, and I joined in, spotting ambiguities in the text that he hadn't addressed and converting them into my own visual puns. This is particularly evident in the illustration of Alice falling down the rabbit hole. It was the very last illustration I made, and I hadn't intended to make it at all. As with all texts by other authors, I was reluctant to illustrate the most descriptive passages, and the fall down the rabbit hole is one of the most dramatic, well-described episodes in the book. But in the end, the distribution of the illustrations meant that an additional painting was required for this part of the book. The only narrative material at this point was the fall down the rabbit hole, so I had little choice but to illustrate it. Ultimately, it was as well that I did make this painting at the very end of the project, because it was an important illustration which required me to be completely settled in the feel of the book. By the time I made the painting I was comfortable with the quasi-surrealist approach I had adopted, and was over my early reservations about the project. As a result, I think it is one of the best illustrations in the book.

Alice is shown, mid-fall, in the centre of the painting, but the most interesting parts of the picture are the items that she passes on her descent. As the text dictates,

Right: *Alice's Adventures in Wonderland,* Julia MacRae Books, 1988

cat's feeding bowl containing a cricket bat. It is a visual pun that pays tribute to dream logic, while at the same time acknowledging the author's predilection for word play.

The frontispiece is the other illustration worthy of mention. At the time the book was published, I was interviewed over the phone for the *Observer*. The interviewer enjoyed spotting my hidden references, and one of the things he had noticed about the frontispiece was my inclusion of the white rabbit in the picture. When he mentioned this, I had no idea what he was talking about, but when I looked at the illustration I saw that the shimmer on the river's surface did indeed form the rough shape of a rabbit's head. I don't know how this happened. It may have been a coincidence; it may have been that I was so immersed in the book that I was seeing white rabbits everywhere; it may have been a subconscious decision. Whatever the case, accidents like this delight me, and long may they continue to happen.

the walls of the rabbit hole are lined with cupboards and bookshelves. On the shelves are all sorts of peculiarities, some of which relate to the thoughts that Carroll describes. These items were prime subjects for the final, improvisatory part of the painting process. As I painted, I allowed my mind to wander in much the same way that Alice's does, and the items on the shelves are the result of our combined reveries.

In the text, Carroll reflects on the nonsensical rhymes and word sequences that Alice contemplates as she falls. Among her ruminations is the question, 'Do cats eat bats?' In the illustration, I painted a

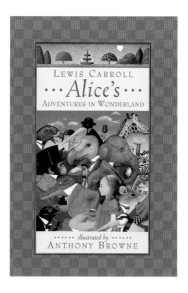

Above, right and opposite:
Alice's Adventures in Wonderland,
Julia MacRae Books, 1988

Chapter Eleven

Journeys

Journeys are a prominent theme in my work, perhaps because they are a prominent theme in my life.

Since I have been successful abroad, my work has been exhibited in many different countries, and I feel privileged to have been invited to talk about my books with children and adults all over the world. Among the places where my work has been exhibited are the Tamayo Museum in Mexico, the Art Institute of Chicago, Bogotá in Colombia, Caracas in Venezuela, Los Angeles, Japan, South Korea, Taiwan, Germany, and many different parts of France.

I have fond memories of all these places, but of all the regions I have visited Latin America occupies the most special place in my heart. Apart from the reception of my work, which is staggeringly positive, the reason I love visiting Latin America is that the people are the warmest, friendliest, happiest and most vital people I have encountered.

The very first time I visited Mexico, I was astonished by every aspect of its culture. The trip was organized by my then editor at Fondo de Cultura Económica, Daniel Goldin, and since that incredible initiation, Daniel has continued to organize exhibitions of my work throughout that part of the world. He has shown me some of the greatest sights I will ever see, and has contributed a huge amount to making my books successful in his home land of Mexico and elsewhere in Latin America. But aside from the debt that I owe him for the publicity he has generated, he is also a good man and I value his friendship and advice very highly. Since Daniel moved on, Fondo have continued to support and promote my work with great enthusiasm, and recently invited me on a fascinating trip to meet the people of Chile and Argentina.

The first exhibition at the Tamayo Museum in Mexico City was breathtaking. I have never seen anything quite like it. It was a massive exhibition, for which my paintings were only a small part of the magnificent display. What the Mexicans had created was essentially an art theme park – an 'Anthony Browne World' of sculptures, installations and large-scale models of the characters from my books.

Even before I saw it, I felt honoured to be exhibited in one of the world's great museums, which houses paintings by the likes of Picasso and Francis Bacon. It is a testament to Mexico's passion for picture books that one of its most prestigious museums was prepared to hold an exhibition in honour of a children's book illustrator . . . and a foreign one at that. But nothing could have prepared me for the astonishing amount of work, commitment, imagination and skill that was put into the project.

The opening of the exhibition was turned into a whole day of festivities. Contributing to the gaiety were musicians, dancers, actors and storytellers. The President of Mexico's wife opened the 'event'. There was an incredible air of ebullience. It was a reaction that seemed absurdly exuberant at the time, but I have since come to realize that it was simply the attitude of a people who love life and aren't shy to celebrate what they are passionate about. I was completely overwhelmed.

The exhibition was elaborately designed. Much of the museum had been divided into a network of rooms, and as one walked into each room one

Chapter opener: *Silly Billy*, Walker Books, 2006

Above: 'El Mundo de Anthony Browne' exhibition, 1996

entered a different book. For example, one of the rooms was devoted to Willy (undoubtedly the Mexicans' favourite of my characters), and was done up to look like the boxing ring from *Willy the Wimp*. It was brilliantly authentic. To make the ring they had brought in real canvas, ropes and boxing paraphernalia. Life-size hand-painted figures of Willy and his 'opponents' were dancing in the centre. Entering this familiar tableau was an odd but thrilling experience: it felt exactly like stepping inside the book.

The other rooms were equally spectacular. The *Alice's Adventures in Wonderland* experience mimicked that of Alice herself, requiring the spectator to walk along a strange corridor before entering a room full of Wonderland references, moving on a conveyor belt. There was a *Tunnel* room too, which looked like a forest, and there was a real tunnel to crawl along, just like the one in the book.

The exhibition 'guides' were in fact storytellers. The original illustrations were displayed on the outside of each themed room, and the first thing the storyteller did was show these to the children and tell them the corresponding story. He or she then assigned various parts to the children and took them into the room to act out a play of the story, using the fantastic scenery and props that were on hand.

All the artwork created for the exhibition was totally original. Everything was handmade and hand-painted; nothing was blown up or mechanically reproduced, and everything on display was a genuine

Opposite and above: 'El Mundo de Anthony Browne' exhibition, 1996

work of art by a group of exceptionally skilled and dedicated craftspeople. The exhibition was phenomenal in every way.

After its success at the Tamayo Museum, Daniel was instrumental in developing similar exhibitions in Colombia and Venezuela. I was lucky enough to see both. It was like a dream: everywhere I went I was surrounded by wonderful, beautiful people who loved my work. The unadulterated joy that the Latin Americans expressed in response to my books instantly seemed to justify everything I had ever done. It was the most incredible feeling.

Whether the response would be quite so jubilant had I not created Willy remains questionable. For some reason, Willy resonates with the Latin American people like no other character; there seems to be

something in their temperament that is embodied by the humble chimpanzee.

Latin America is very special to me for many reasons. I will remember it mainly for the wonderful people and the exhibitions of my books, but it was also the setting for the proudest work-related moment of my life. The Hans Christian Andersen Award is an international prize, presented biennially to an author and an illustrator for their lifetime contributions to world children's literature. I was nominated in 1998 and didn't win. No British illustrator had ever won the prize, and the only British author to do so was Eleanor Farjeon, way back in 1956. The prize is issued by the International Board on Books for Young People (IBBY). Every two years, each IBBY country puts forward an author and an illustrator for the prize. The jury then assembles to decide on the winners, and a huge conference is held to present the award. It is a massive honour that has been dubbed the Nobel Prize for children's literature.

I was nominated for the second time in 2000, and had no reason to expect a different result. When the president of IBBY phoned to tell me I had won, I felt dizzy. It is the greatest honour that can be bestowed on a children's book illustrator, and the news was almost too much to handle. I had never dreamed of winning the Hans Christian Andersen. I had won awards before: the Kate Greenaway Medal twice, for *Gorilla* and *Zoo*, the Kurt Maschler Award three times, two Dutch Silver Pencil Awards and two Youth Literature Prizes in Germany. I had also won a silver medal from the American Association of Illustrators. What makes the Hans Christian Andersen medal particularly special is the fact that it is an award for a lifetime of work, as opposed to an individual book. The award is 'in recognition of a lasting contribution to children's literature', so it feels almost like a validation of one's entire career.

The final accolade to mention (I promise I'll move on after this!) wasn't a prize as such. It was 2005, and I was involved in a scheme organized by the School of Education at Kingston University, called Books Alive. They wanted to turn *Voices in the Park* into an interactive, multimedia book which would be used in the teaching of literacy. At first I was a little anxious about the project – perhaps it is my age, but the words 'interactive' and 'multimedia'

Above, top and opposite: 'El Mundo de Anthony Browne' exhibition, 1996
Above: receiving the Andersen medal and diploma from IBBY President Tayo Shima, 2000

have always instilled a slight sense of distrust, especially when used in the context of picture books. But the Books Alive people proved to be very understanding, and I was soon convinced that their endeavours would be nothing but beneficial to children's appreciation of picture books. I worked quite closely with Books Alive on the project, helping to promote the scheme and inspire the children, and was later very honoured to be given a Doctorate in Education by Kingston University.

One of the most pleasing things I have learned from my travels is that picture books are being kept alive in other parts of the world. British picture book publishers have been panicking for some time now about the perceived moribund state of the industry. Computer games and DVDs are commonly blamed, but these things don't seem to have affected the sales of children's novels. Partly thanks to the remarkable Harry Potter phenomenon, more children are reading now than for a long time, and tremendous though this is, it seems to have inspired a worrying trend among parents. Children in this country are being encouraged to read pictureless books younger and younger, and picture books are being pushed aside in favour of more overtly 'advancing' novels. Perhaps the increased competition and earlier exams in schools are responsible, but parents seem to be nudging their offspring towards an earlier graduation from intellectual infancy: the 'picture books are for babies' mentality. This is nonsense. Children have a very acute sense of visual awareness, which needs to be nurtured with great care. At an early age, their visual education is just as important as their literary education, and the transition stage during which they move from a visual to a more word-based response is a delicate period that shouldn't be accelerated.

In many other parts of the world picture books are still thriving. I am thankful for the foreign rights teams at Random House and Walker Books, and for my magnificent team of foreign publishers who have succeeded in broadening my international appeal, because the foreign attitude to picture books is far more encouraging. Nowhere is this more evident than in France and Mexico, and I am very lucky to have been embraced by the markets in both countries.

But not all is lost in Britain. Regardless of their parents' attitudes, the response from British children is as encouraging as ever. Moreover, the decline in sales doesn't seem to have affected the attitude in many schools, which have remained supportive of picture books. Schoolchildren are encouraged to write to authors, and I get hundreds of letters every year. They are copious and varied: drawings, stories, ideas for books, photographs . . . Even though replying to the letters can be laborious, I am still delighted to receive them. The responses from children have helped and inspired me over the years. The most overt instance of this was the group of Dutch schoolchildren who helped with the creation of *My Brother*, but even when they don't inspire me directly, children constantly replenish my enthusiasm for picture books. I invariably come away from schools feeling more confident about what I do and why I do it. I enjoy talking to children, and wherever I go they are responsive, interested and, above all, interesting.

My trips abroad have produced some wonderful experiences. The warmth and generosity I have encountered are staggering, and people's willingness to present me with gifts means that I rarely return home empty-handed. On one occasion I was giving a talk at a book event in Bogotá, Colombia. In typical Latin American fashion it was a huge, grand affair with hundreds of children and adults reacting with enthusiastic celebration. At one point an announcement was made in Spanish and a tiny old Colombian-Indian woman was helped onto the platform. She could barely walk, but she was determined to reach me. She tottered across the stage and gave me a handmade cloth doll of Willy. She had made it herself. It was beautifully crafted, and the detail was incredible. His hair was parted in the middle and his sleeveless jumper was decorated with the trademark pattern. It was a lovely thought that while I had been in my studio in England, this tiny, aged woman, thousands of miles away in another land, another culture, had been creating this beautiful gift for me. Apart from one unfortunate incident with my friend's dog, Willy has sat in my studio unperturbed ever since. He seems to enjoy watching me work.

On my next trip to Colombia, for the Hans Christian Andersen presentation, I was presented

Below: Willy doll and wooden toy

Overleaf: *Silly Billy*, Walker Books, 2006

with a carved wooden toy of Willy as an acrobat. I thought I knew Willy very well, but I had no idea he was so agile! He hangs by his arms from a string attached to what looks like a set of rugby posts (at least it does to me); if you squeeze the posts from the bottom, he performs a flip over the string. It was carved by a young Colombian man, and I felt humbled to think that Willy was considered for the subject.

The people of Australia have also been extremely generous to me. The first time I went I was handed out as the 'prize' to a school that had won a competition for a project based on my books. I was rewarded with an amazing portfolio of work by the children. The most memorable piece was a little boy's flick-book, which told the story of all the children posting the package of work to the competition organizers. It was superb.

Also in the portfolio were dozens of drawings: self-portraits, characters from my books and imaginary scenarios taking place in the world of Anthony Browne. This has been a common theme over the years: a lot of children produce work within the context of my 'world'. It is, perhaps unsurprisingly, a world characterized by surreal landscapes and a large number of gorillas, not unlike Planet of the Apes, I suppose!

The second time I went to Australia I was again sent to a prize-winning school for the day, this time right in the heart of the outback. It was an unforgettable experience. I was flown out in a tiny plane, before being driven to the school in a four-by-four vehicle. From the moment I arrived I was treated

like an alien . . . or a pop star. The children had never seen a picture-book author before; perhaps not many of them had seen a foreigner, so I was highly exotic! Once they were used to me, however, they were as responsive as any children I have encountered. They were thoroughly deserving of the prize, for their work was magnificent. My visit was rewarded with a private viewing of the musical they had produced, which featured various characters from my books, and the context was again 'the world of Anthony Browne'. For a group of children who knew so little of the world outside their own, it was amazing how much they knew about mine.

I am impressed by the Australian attitude to picture books. Without the wild, celebratory spirit of Latin America, there is nonetheless a respect, dedication and seriousness that is pleasing to see. The Australians share my opinion that picture books aren't just for young children. There are real efforts in place in Australia and New Zealand (which I have also visited) to target children over the age of eight, which are succeeding in generating a greater respect for picture books among parents. The tendency to enforce premature literary progress doesn't seem to be part of their culture.

One thing my travels (both domestic and abroad) have taught me is that children are the same all over the world. The details they find in the pictures; the comments they make; the things they find funny or scary: they are the same wherever I go. I think one of the reasons picture books are enjoyed internationally is that children generally are without prejudice. In the past I have worried about isolating readers because of cultural disparities between nationalities, but I have since learned that such concerns are needless. Cultural differences don't really exist between young children; at least, the children don't seem to be aware of them. The notion of difference is something we develop as we get older. We are eventually taught that people from other countries 'do things differently', but young children find this impossible to understand, because they aren't any different.

I have been published abroad for a long time, but the escalation of my international appeal is a fairly recent occurrence. As a result I have been invited to more countries in recent years, and this has undoubtedly affected my work. *Silly Billy* owes a lot to Latin America, but my Lancastrian mother should be equally credited.

On one of my trips to Mexico I was given a box of worry dolls. They were beautiful objects: hand-made and decorated in typically bright Mexican colours. There were approximately ten tiny dolls, all individuals of either gender, dressed in different clothes. I'm not sure how the man who gave me the gift knew about the worry gene which has passed through the Browne family for generations (perhaps it is betrayed in my books somehow), but it could not have been more appropriate.

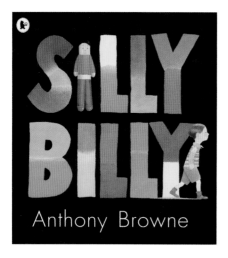

Above: *Silly Billy,* Walker Books, 2006
Opposite: dummy for *Silly Billy,* Walker Books, 2006

The donor said that all I needed to do was tell the dolls my worries before I went to sleep, leave them under my pillow overnight and my worries would be gone by the morning. I was touched and encouraged. If the gift really would lead to a life without worries, then I was for ever in his debt. But before I got home I realized that there was someone who would benefit from the worry dolls even more than me: the greatest worrier I have ever known, my mother.

Our Doris was delighted with the dolls. For the first few nights they were a great success. During this time she was noticeably less worried. Then one morning she came downstairs with a familiar look on her face. She was clearly worried.

'I'm worried, Our Tony,' she said.

'What about?' I asked.

'I've lost the worry dolls.'

In the book, Billy worries constantly. He worries about hats, shoes, clouds, rain and giant birds. His parents try to console him by saying that none of the things he worries about could actually happen, and (to use a line that constantly echoed through my own children's bedrooms when they were very young), 'It's just your imagination.' Although Billy's parents have good intentions, the words are no more effective with Billy than they were with my son, whose response was invariably, 'I know, but I don't want an imagination; I want to stop worrying!'

One night Billy goes to stay with his grandma. One of the things he worries about is staying at other people's houses, and after a period of being unable to sleep, he decides to tell his grandma all about it. She gives Billy some worry dolls. 'They'll do all the worrying for you while you sleep,' she says.

Just like Our Doris, the worry dolls work for Billy for a few nights. But after that, Billy starts to worry again. He worries about the worry dolls themselves. How unfair to burden them with all his worries!

The next day, Billy takes the problem into his own hands by making worry dolls for the worry dolls. Everybody sleeps well after that and Billy doesn't worry much at all.

I originally wanted to use Willy for the book. In many ways he was a natural choice. He is, after all, the chimp who worries about treading on tiny insects as he walks. I even made a dummy with Willy as the protagonist, calling it *Willy the Worrier.* Although I have never stated Willy's age, the story was definitely about a young child, so I made it clear in the dummy that Willy was recalling his early child-hood when he was still wearing short trousers!

I showed the dummy to my inspired editor, Denise Johnstone-Burt. She liked the story very much, but thought the idea was wasted on Willy. Her view was that the *Willy* series had become so established that the character alone was enough to attach superficial value to a book. In other words, *Willy the Worrier* would be 'just another *Willy* book'. It is ironic that such a humble, introverted character as Willy was considered iconic enough to overshadow a good story.

At the time I was appalled by Denise's suggestion. Of course the story was about Willy; I had drawn him in every picture and it seemed impossible to imagine the book without him. Denise suggested, quite reasonably, that I try using a different animal for the protagonist . . . a rabbit, perhaps; but I, in my stubbornness, thought it was the most ridicu-lous idea I had ever heard. I dread to think what I might have done to a rabbit had it crossed my path

on the way home from that meeting.

I went back to the dummy and drew over the pictures of Willy. As with *Voices in the Park*, I had little idea what I intended; I was relying on the hope that something interesting would 'appear'. Willy became not a rabbit but a little boy. Billy remains very similar to Willy in every respect, except that he is human. He is dressed the same as Willy; he has the same hairstyle; he has the same big ears; he walks in the same hunched manner. I like to imagine that, had Willy created the book, he might have humanized his protagonist in the way that I have tended to simianize mine. For me, Billy and Willy are interchangeable, and I view *Silly Billy* as a *Willy* book in all but title.

I researched the book by investigating the most common childhood fears. They vary from age group to age group, but the fears that prevailed were of the dark; being lost or on one's own; monsters/fantasy creatures; the death of oneself or a parent; and thunderstorms. I intended to use these in the

book, because I wanted as many readers as possible to identify with Billy. But then I remembered how sensitive and impressionable I was as a young child, and how my own children's fears were easily triggered by suggestion. The last thing I wanted was for a child with no fear of death to develop one after reading about Billy's experience. In the end I made Billy's worries ridiculous; things that couldn't possibly happen. Apart from the giant bird, which admittedly borders on terrifying, they are about mundane things that are unlikely to sap sleep from even the most imaginative children. Unusual though many of my children's worries were, I don't remember them tormenting themselves over the thought of shoes climbing up the wall.

To emphasize the impossibility of Billy's worries, I drew them in black and white or monochrome, so that they were clearly separate from reality.

I mentioned that Our Doris was the primary model for the worrying theme. What was distinctive about her worries was that they were always about other people. Our Doris proved that there is a very close relationship between worrying and caring, and I think that when worries become cares, it shows a certain emotional maturity in the individual. At the start of *Silly Billy*, Billy's worries are very inward-looking and self-concerned: he is worried about things that might happen to him. By the end of the story, however, he is no longer worried about himself; he has turned his worries outwards, focusing on the worry dolls instead. In a sense, he has grown up; he has learned to convert his worries into cares

for others. I wanted the message of the book not to be that people shouldn't worry at all. Everybody worries, but it is only the kindest among us who are able to channel their worries into concerns for other people.

Child psychiatrists often encourage children to draw their anxieties in an attempt to exorcize them. The process of manifesting the worries into something outwardly visual can help to purge them from the child's consciousness. This is essentially what Billy does by making the worry dolls at the end of the book.

The colours in *Silly Billy* are clearly influenced by my trips to Latin America. Mexico in particular has its own special brand of brilliant, rich colours that are in keeping with the vitality of its people. Gradually over time, the colours of Latin America have infiltrated my work, and Silly Billy represents the culmination of my changed colour palette.

Opposite and above:
Silly Billy, Walker Books, 2006

Chapter Twelve
Fairy Tales

I first devised *Into the Forest* when I was working on *The Tunnel*. The original plot for *The Tunnel* was very similar to *Into the Forest*, but for some reason I abandoned it. It wasn't the book I wanted to create at the time. I rewrote the story, developed *The Tunnel*, and didn't think about the original plot again for years.

Then, in 2003, I went to a writers' retreat in Denmark with a view to turning an idea into a book. I had been confident about the idea before I left, but within a morning of being at the retreat I turned against it (I suddenly realized that it wouldn't work), and was presented with the problem of what to do for the next ten days. Beautiful and serene though the place was, there was nothing to do there except write, and I had nothing to write about!

I wandered around, searching hopelessly for inspiration, surrounded only by other writers whose scribbling fists tauntingly proved that they had already found it at the retreat; perhaps one or two of them had 'found themselves', who knows?

Every evening we would all meet to discuss what we had written during the day. I, being one of the few writers whose primary language was English, was expected to talk quite lucidly about my day's work, but all I was able to impart was my appreciation of the trees, which were lovely.

The retreat was in the middle of a forest. It was snowing while I was there, and the snow-covered forest early in the morning was one of the most beautiful walking environments I have ever known. It was on one of these perfect walks that I started to think about the story I had written years before, which had evolved into *The Tunnel*. The forest reminded me of this story, and, by association,

I reminded myself of the protagonist, who has to walk through the forest on the way to his grandma's house. Back then I called the story *Where Are You, Dad?* and in the isolation of the Danish retreat I quickly rewrote it in my head. *Into the Forest* was born.

The story is about a little boy who wakes up one morning to find that his father is mysteriously absent. His mother doesn't seem to know where he has gone, so the boy posts little notes all over the house: *Come home, Dad*. One day his mother asks him to take a cake to his poorly grandma. The journey has two possible routes: the long way around, or the short way through the forest.

His mother warns him to go the long way in order to avoid the forest, but – staying faithful to an established fairytale tradition of miscreants,

including Jack the Giant Killer, Sleeping Beauty and Red Riding Hood – he disregards his mother's warning and goes into the forest. On the way to Grandma's house he encounters various fairytale characters. Although none of them are named, the familiar cast includes ghostly incarnations of Hansel and Gretel, Jack and Goldilocks. The boy walks on until he finds a red coat hanging from a tree. He is cold, so he puts it on, but immediately starts to feel scared. His fear turns into terror, and he breaks into a run in an effort to evade his imaginary (quite possibly lupine) pursuer.

Eventually he arrives at Grandma's house. A strange voice answers his knock on the door, which he pushes open nervously, not knowing what to expect in his grandma's bed.

But the figure in the nightgown proves to be his grandma, who greets him with the same strange voice as before; it is distorted because she is severely blocked-up by a heavy cold. To complete the happy ending, who should come out of the shadows but Dad? He has been looking after his ill mother all this time. The boy and his father return home together, where they are welcomed by a happy and smiling Mum.

The story is evidently influenced by fairy tales (most notably *Little Red Riding Hood*), but it also draws on a real childhood experience. I was about six years old and my grandparents were supposed to come to our house for Sunday lunch. I had a new plastic rifle that I was keen to show them at the earliest opportunity, so my parents told me I could walk to the bus stop and meet them straight off the bus. I got to the bus stop, rifle cocked at the ready, but the bus didn't come, so I decided to walk the two or three miles to their house all on my own. For the first part of the adventure I felt pleased with myself. I looked great with the gun, and walking to my grandparents' house was the kind of thing that grown-ups did! But soon it started to snow, and the road became less familiar. Before I knew it I was lost, freezing cold and terrified.

I eventually found my way there. It turned out that Dad had suspected what had happened and set off in his car to look for me. But there were two ways of getting from our house to the Red Lion (where my grandparents still lived): I had walked one way and Dad had driven the other, so we had

Chapter opener: *Into the Forest*, Walker Books, 2004

Previous spread, above and opposite:
Into the Forest, Walker Books, 2004

missed each other. He was already there by the time I arrived. The rifle was still fearsome in my hands, but there were tears streaming down my face.

So *Into the Forest* was partly based on my experience as a child, and was partly yet another attempt to illustrate a fairy tale – something I had been trying to do again ever since *Hansel and Gretel* was published in 1981. It is an endeavour that, despite lasting over twenty years, has only ever achieved semi-fruition. *Into the Forest* is about as close as I have come, but despite numerous references to the works of Grimm, Andersen and Perrault, the story is still ultimately my own. It could be said that the work is a compilation of fairy tales, encompassed within a modern story, and I have used the forest (the most prevailing of fairytale landscapes) as the setting for the compilation.

There had to be a reason why fairy tales are on the boy's mind as he enters the forest, so before he sets off he tells us, 'I love Grandma. She always tells such fantastic stories,' suggesting that Grandma is responsible for his preoccupation with fairy tales. The boy's fascination with fiction, coupled with the fact that the illustrations of the fairytale characters are drawn in pencil (whereas he is painted in watercolour), enshrouds the whole sequence of events in ambiguity. Are they real or just part of his imagination? Whether he imagines them or not, a more direct reading interprets the black and white parts of the illustrations as the fairytale world, and the coloured parts as reality.

The protagonist is a descendant of Rose in *The Tunnel*, whose venture into the forest was also made more colourful by her fascination with fairy tales. In many ways, *Into the Forest* is a variation of *The Tunnel*, and I make no attempt to hide its close relationship. Some of the forest illustrations are intentionally very similar. As with the earlier book, I played the Shape Game with the trees, and as the boy progresses through the forest there are more and more fairytale motifs woven into their elaborate tapestry. It is notable that as he first enters the forest, the trees are very ordinary. Just like me as I set off for my grandparents' house with the plastic gun, he feels brave at this point; of course he is big enough to take the short cut. As he gets deeper into the forest,

Above and opposite:
Into the Forest, Walker Books, 2004

however, his bravery dwindles while his imagination gets the better of him. Before long there are shapes and symbols everywhere. Flicking through the book, a few that stand out are the giant's club, the gingerbread cottage, the spinning wheel and the tower with a prodigious plait of hair dangling from its upper porthole.

It is clear that the boy has an active imagination, making it debatable whether or not the events in the forest actually occur. But even the events outside the forest carry their own mystery. At the very beginning of the book, the boy is 'wakened by a terrible sound'. We assume that he's referring to the

electric storm that is visible from the window, but the next morning Dad has gone, and Mum is mysteriously reticent. The subtle implication is that the 'terrible sound' could have been Mum and Dad arguing – a notion that is reinforced by the one-legged toy soldier on the boy's bedroom floor in the opening illustration, which at once alludes to Hans Christian Andersen's story, *The Steadfast Tin Soldier*, and also evokes thoughts of conflict.

It is a common technique to juxtapose real-life problems with retreat into fantasy. Perhaps everything that happens to the protagonist in the forest is in some way related to the events at home. When he arrives at Grandma's house, Dad is there. It becomes clear that at least one of the reasons he was away from home was to look after his sick mother. If there was another reason, it has apparently been resolved by the time father and son arrive home, because they are both greeted by Mum, who is smiling.

In some ways then, *Into the Forest* isn't just the fairy tale that it seems to be. Alongside the fantastical events in the forest there is a curious subplot which is rooted in social realism. In a society in which one in three marriages ends in divorce, the 'terrible sound' of Mum and Dad arguing is something that a lot of children have to endure. I have tentatively tried to address the issue in *Into the Forest*. Although a lot of my books make 'comments', I don't like to be too forthright with my young readers, and I hope that by diluting the difficult subject in several

units of fairy tale material, I have made it a little easier to swallow.

The protagonist encounters several fairy tale characters in the story, but the encounters are so fleeting that he is unable to develop a relationship with any of them. They remain on the periphery of the story. Although their appearance is generated by the boy's fascination with fairy tale culture, none of them become fully-fledged characters; instead, they maintain a dreamy, half-real quality that is difficult to engage with.

The story begins and ends with real domestic events, and it could be said that reality ultimately triumphs over fantasy. This seems to be the case in a lot of my books. Perhaps the reason I have avoided illustrating a fairy tale for so long is that I am reluctant to throw myself into the fantasy genre. Very few of my books have completely departed from reality, and whenever something fantastical happens, it is usually explained as the product of a character's dream or imagination. With the exception of the *Bear* books, which feature a character who is able to make something materialize simply by drawing it, there are no irrefutable instances of magic or the paranormal in my work. Some might say that my frequent animalization of characters borders on fantasy, but I would disagree. The non-human characters in my books are not magic, talking animals; they are metaphors for real people, which children seem to identify with. I love fairy tales, but I seem to be uncomfortable with the idea of writing about witches, giants and magic spells.

Above: *Into the Forest*, Walker Books, 2004

It is difficult to say where my work is taking me, particularly as my recent ideas have been so disparate; indeed, if any pattern can be deduced from my work, it is that it has become more explorative. In recent years, my books have contrasted quite considerably, involving experimentations in layout (*Willy's Pictures*); preparation (*The Shape Game*); genre (*Into the Forest*); and colour (*Silly Billy*). I have used many different drawing and painting styles throughout my career. My experience designing greetings cards endowed me with a decent repertoire of skills, and consequently the artwork in my books ranges from the hyper-realistic animal portraits in *Zoo* to the cheerful, cartoonish renderings of Willy and co. Watercolour is undoubtedly my preferred medium, but I have occasionally turned to pencil, acrylic and gouache. Several of my books feature different styles at different points in the story – a device to serve changes in narrative direction or mood. Until recently, this was most evident in *Voices in the Park*, but *Little Beauty* demonstrates even more variation in the pictures.

Little Beauty was based on two true stories about the same gorilla. A female gorilla at a zoo in California was taught sign language. The experiment was an incredible success, proving much about the gorilla's intellectual capabilities. Koko the gorilla was taught so many signs that she was able to communicate many of her feelings with the keepers at the zoo, and answer most of the questions they asked her. Moreover, she invented some words herself. Her term for 'gorilla' was 'animal person', which I suspect Darwin would find as fascinating as I do.

One day a keeper came to Koko's cage to find that her washbasin had been destroyed. She had ripped it away from the wall and it lay smashed on the floor. The keeper looked at Koko, a bit cross, and signed, 'What happened?'

After a moment's hesitation, Koko signed back to her, 'The keeper did it.'

Whatever the motive behind the gorilla's answer, it is fascinating. It could be that she lied to avoid a reprimand from the keeper; this would suggest that a gorilla's mind is sophisticated enough to invent a lie. Alternatively, perhaps she realized that her claim was so absurd it was impossible for the keeper to believe her. If this was the case, then she could only have been telling a joke, proving that she had a sense of humour! Either way, it is amazing.

In the other story I heard about Koko, she was given a kitten to see how a gorilla would respond to the concept of keeping a pet. Koko loved the kitten dearly. For a long time she cared for it, played with it, and was as tender an owner as could be imagined. But one night the kitten escaped from the cage and was killed on a nearby road. Koko was devastated, and mourned the kitten's death for days. It isn't such a light-hearted story as the first, but it does go even further to illustrate the similarity between gorillas and human beings.

I revised the details of these two stories later, but the creation of Little Beauty was in fact the result of me mis-remembering the stories and combining them in my head. The book is consequently an amalgamation of the two stories, with crucially altered details. The gorilla in Little Beauty is male. Just like Koko, he is versed in sign language and given a pet kitten, Beauty, whom he loves. One day he destroys his television set in a fit of rage (he is watching King Kong), and when the keeper asks him what happened, he blames it on the kitten.

The ending posed a problem, because a lot of people thought it approved a casual attitude to lying: the gorilla blames his aggressive act on somebody else, but it's OK because it's funny. I wasn't implying anything of the sort. Just because this particular gorilla lied (or perhaps told a joke) on this particular occasion doesn't mean it is acceptable to lie under any circumstances. I know that most children are astute enough to realize this, but a lot of people were uneasy about the perceived ambiguity of the 'message'. I wrestled with the problem for a long time and it caused me much grief, but I eventually decided to have the kitten flex her muscles in response to the gorilla's answer. Beauty is a passive character throughout the story, and by pretending to admit to smashing the TV she makes it clear that the whole incident can be laughed off. I hope that this makes the story more about friendship than dishonesty.

'Little Beauty' is the name of the kitten, but the title of the book also refers to a fairy tale – the gorilla, the implied Beast. The allusion is substantiated by the recurrence of roses throughout the book.

I decided to set the story in a domestic environment. The original gorilla, Koko, lived in a zoo,

but she had a washbasin in her cage, and was in possession of very human abilities to communicate, so I placed my gorilla in a domestic setting to exaggerate his human attributes. As far as the reader is concerned, the gorilla lives in something like a glass-fronted house, complete with an armchair, a standard lamp and William Morris wallpaper.

The drawing and painting styles vary throughout the book. It seems to be an unwritten rule of the profession that all the illustrations within a picture book should be drawn in the same style. Few people have defied this rule, and I'm not sure why. I tried to challenge it as often as I could in *Little Beauty*. The first time we see the gorilla, he is painted in painful detail: every hair is discernible. After that, I varied the degree of looseness; sometimes parts of him are captured in fine detail, while other parts are represented by large splodges of watercolour.

Elsewhere in the book, his whole form is very roughly drawn in pencil. There were no narrative reasons behind the different styles: I was simply obeying my instincts.

The picture of the keepers is painted with tightly knit cross-hatching and – just as I exaggerated the gorilla's genetic proximity to human beings – I brought to mind the origin of the species by emphasizing the male keepers' body hair.

Some of the pictures are incredibly rough. The most dramatic departure from my typical detailed style is represented by the double-page illustration of the gorilla carrying Beauty, accompanied by the text, 'And they were happy.' Although the floral wallpaper in the background is meticulous, the two figures in the foreground are the product of a five-minute sketch. The reason for this speedy execution was not laziness. Contrary to my very tight, attentive approach to illustration, I have always admired the loose, flowing style of drawing. I think that quick sketching is a healthy practice which can produce the most expressive results. I still remember my college tutor Derek Hyatt's lesson that all art should communicate; the child-like method of getting a drawing down as quickly and simply as possible is often the most effective way of achieving that. Ask a child to draw a table and he/she will, in an instant, produce an image that says everything necessary about a table. Ask a professional artist to do the same, and he/she may take weeks to produce an image that

Opposite and above:
Little Beauty, Walker Books, 2008

is no more effective at communicating its subject.

I find myself using the child's approach when I produce my dummies. In the case of *Little Beauty*, I was so pleased with the expressiveness I had achieved in the dummy drawing of the gorilla carrying Beauty that I was reluctant to recreate it in a more thorough, less spontaneous, less joyous form. I have drawn hundreds of gorillas in my lifetime, and although it was produced without any visual reference or attention to detail, this was one of the most gorilla-like gorillas I had ever drawn. I had simply concentrated on what it was I was trying to communicate; not whether the drawing was any good or not. Concerns about the quality of a picture can detract from the clarity of its communicative attributes, and in the absence of these concerns I had produced an image that said everything I needed to say. Moreover, the flowing quality of the drawing effectively illustrated the first real instance of movement in the book. Even the emotion of the characters seemed to be enhanced.

I would have preferred to use the dummy version in the final book, but, because I had drawn it so small, simply to blow the image up would be ill-advised. So I drew the image again on a larger scale, trying to recreate the lucidity and ease of the original drawing. I think I managed it quite well.

The illustration might have had a jarring effect in the context of the book had I not made the previous picture of the gorilla feeding honey to the kitten fairly loose as well. I also made the wallpaper in the background as detailed as possible in an effort

to control the contextual impact of the unusual illustration.

The illustrations for *Little Beauty* are less complicated than they are for some of my books, but there are a few details worthy of mention. In the illustration of the gorilla swinging from the lamp, I have incorporated a hidden warning to children: 'Don't try this at home!' The lampshade and bulb are drawn in an unrealistic, diagrammatic style, implying that the light itself isn't real; the gorilla isn't really performing this dangerous stunt. The painting on the wall is Bruegel's 'Landscape with the Fall of Icarus'. Beauty helpfully points to the figure of the failed aviator (his legs form a tiny part of the painting as he plunges into the sea). The kitten seems to remind both the gorilla and the reader of the perils involved in attempting such heroics, and perhaps prophesy a fall of another kind.

The experimentation in style continues through-out the book. The illustrations are generally colourful, particularly in the early part of the book when the gorilla is content. When he gets angry, the illustration is drawn in aggressive charcoal, which is hardly softened by the plain red wash. The drawing is sketchy once again, my intention being to produce

a less pretty, more dynamic image.

Similarly, in the final picture of Beauty flexing her muscles, she reveals a new side of her character, so I drew her with the same loose, intuitive approach that I used for the picture of the gorilla carrying her.

I took liberties with virtually every picture. Each time the gorilla appears he is slightly changed. The illustrations are dictated more by expression than representation, and the gorilla was a vehicle for this reactive form of drawing as opposed to a consistently real character.

The final picture shows a white rose and a red rose, and I played the Shape Game by hiding the faces of the two friends in the petals. The roses substantiate the allusion to *Beauty and the Beast* that is implied throughout the book, not only in the name of the kitten.

My next book was a retelling of *Goldilocks and the Three Bears*, called *Me and You*.

I had always thought that Goldilocks should feel aggrieved at her representation in the original story. The assumption is that she trespasses on the bears' property, steals their food and breaks their possessions for no other reason than to appease her own greed. I tried to imagine a back-story to the fairy tale. Perhaps she didn't just break into the bears' house for fun: perhaps she really was in distress and in need of food and shelter. In most tellings of the story, it is the bears with whom we are encouraged to sympa-thize, but I thought it was about time the tale was told from another perspective.

My first thought was to tell the story twice. The first half of the book was to be dedicated to the bears' interpretation. Apart from the modernization of the setting, and the bears' contemporary human attire, the narrative was fairly traditional. The bears live a very comfortable, middle-class life and they arrive home one day to discover a 'horrible, dirty little child' fleeing their golden house, leaving a trail of broken chairs and empty porridge bowls in her wake. They are appalled, and fail to imagine that the little girl might be starving or distressed.

The second half of the book was to be Goldilocks's interpretation, which would explain the circumstances under which she was forced to 'victimise' the bears.

I started the book with these intentions, but soon realized that it didn't work. The whole book was far too bleak. After the opening, which focused on the bears' wealth and complacency, the book ended with Goldilocks wandering off into the dark winter night, with no clue to her fate. Yes, it was encouraging a different reading of the traditional fairy tale, but how did I expect children to respond to an ending of such emptiness?

The format was also a concern. The sudden trans-ferral of narrator at the halfway point seemed like a clumsy strategy.

What to do with the book posed a big problem for a long time, but I eventually got help from my brilliant French editor, Isabel Finkenstaedt. She suggested that it would be better to tell the two stories simultaneously, with the bears' version (specifically the baby bear's) on the right-hand page

Opposite: *Little Beauty,* Walker Books, 2008
Below: *Me and You,* Doubleday, 2010

Opposite, above and right:
Me and You, Doubleday, 2010

of each spread and Goldilocks's on the left. She also suggested that Goldilocks's story be told silently, with no text accompanying the illustrations. It was a fantastic idea. As we read the two stories Goldilocks is always one step ahead of the bears until they meet in Baby Bear's bedroom. I also decided to make the ending a lot more hopeful and perhaps suggest that Goldilocks at least has something that the bears don't possess.

I started again with the pictures but ran into some predictable trouble drawing the bears.

No matter how hard I tried I couldn't give them the character I wanted. They were too bland, too much like any old bears in any old picture book.

Reluctantly I tried changing them and – yes, you guessed it – they morphed into gorillas! How incredibly annoying. At this stage I hadn't found the title, but *Goldilocks and the Three Gorillas* sounded ridiculous. I played around with their faces until they were a sort of cross between a bear and a gorilla – a bearilla? But although they looked interestingly strange (at least to me), I felt that it wouldn't do. By changing medium into soft coloured pencil I finally found the comfortable, golden images of the bears I wanted, and they each revealed something of their character in their appearance.

For Goldilocks I decided to try to reflect her life by painting her and her world in dark brown colours, to tell her story almost like a graphic novel, and suggest her outsider status by giving her reddish gold hair and glasses. The book was dedicated to all the underdogs in the world like Goldilocks.

Despite the stark differences of viewpoint, I have tried to suggest a connection between Goldilocks and Baby Bear. Embedded in their parallel stories is an unspoken affinity between them.

Chapter Thirteen

Playing the
Shape Game

I hope to continue making picture books for as long as I can. Assuming that my health holds out, the only potential threat I can foresee is the threat to picture books in general. I am concerned about the industry for a number of reasons. Cutbacks in library spending, cutbacks in the numbers of picture books stocked by the major book chains, the threat of the e-book, computer games, TV and DVDs, as well as the apparent decline in the popularity of picture books among parents – these are all concerns of mine.

Many schools do a great job in keeping picture books alive, but there are also those that encourage children to read only excerpts of a book instead of the whole thing. Perhaps it is the pressure of exam success that has made some teachers determined to extract every last ounce of 'learning' from books, for I am getting a lot more questions from children

hoping to find an almost mathematical logic in my material. 'What exactly was magic about Willy's football boots?' 'Was the father in *Gorilla* wearing a gorilla costume? . . . Why did he have a banana sticking out of his pocket?'

My suspicion is that these aren't the children's own questions (they tend to be common to every letter from an entire class); I would guess that the children are encouraged to ask them by their teachers. But what the teachers don't realize is that children are perfectly capable of answering them with their own imaginations, even if their answers aren't the logical ones the teachers were hoping for. I prefer it when the children are allowed to ask what they like in their letters, and even daft questions such as 'Which football team do you support?' or 'Do you have a dog?' are better than the literal, truth-seeking questions of the teachers' preference.

One thing I can say about my career is that I have always tried to make the best picture books I possibly can. I was about to write that to concentrate on making good books as opposed to commercial books is a luxury that I have been able to afford only in recent years, but in actual fact, I have always had this approach. Apart from the *Bear* books, which I produced early in my career as a response to accusations of self-indulgence, it has never been my primary objective to make books that will sell in large quantities. As I have got older and accumulated more books bearing my name, I have become even more concerned about the quality of each one, which partly explains my reduction in pace. I have tried to resist the temptation to dumb down, and consistently try to produce books that I believe in.

My books are unusual – often most rewarding after a little perseverance – and tend not to offer immediate, effortless gratification. Apart from Willy and Bear there are no recurring characters, and there are no TV series or computer games that I can ride on the back of. Thankfully, it is an understanding and knowledgeable group of people I work with, and I am grateful that they have allowed me to carry on producing my own kind of picture books.

In the latter part of this book I have written a lot about my work and little about the other areas of my life. Proud as I am of the books I have made, by far the greatest satisfactions in my life are my two children. No creation for which I am responsible is so brimming with imagination, originality, colour and vitality. The joy, pleasure and inspiration that my

Chapter opener: *Summer Evening*, 2010

Above: Joe and Ellen, 2010

Overleaf: Joe, Anthony and Ellen, 1989

children Joe and Ellen have given me is incomparable, and being a father is more important to me than being a writer/illustrator. It is an accurate cliché that having children changes everything, and my life has been immeasurably enhanced since they became part of it.

As well as helping me to understand more about life in general, Joe and Ellen have helped me to become better at my job. Becoming a father has allowed me to see at first hand what sensitive, intelligent, interested minds children have. Previously when I created my books, I would draw upon my own memories of being a child, as well as the responses from the children I spoke to in schools,

but watching my own children grow up has, in a sense, allowed me to experience childhood for a second time. The fears, anxieties, pleasures and fantasies that I remember from childhood suddenly became much more vivid when Joe and Ellen experienced them.

Their opinions are always valuable and it has been a great privilege for someone in my position to have worked under the influence of their honesty and wisdom. They have offered insight and encouragement. Moreover, they are as interested and encouraging now (they are both 'grown up') as they were when they were very young, and this has taught me that there is no cut-off point with picture-book appreciation. Joe and Ellen have continued to enjoy books throughout their progression into adulthood. Of course, the reading experience has changed for them, but they are still very supportive and helpful, and I frequently look to them for advice.

Becoming a father has reinforced my belief that we underestimate children's abilities. The astuteness that has been shown to me by both my own children and the thousands of schoolchildren I have spoken to over the years has taught me to ignore the few critics who say that my books are too complicated. Children see and understand so much. When they were young, Joe and Ellen spotted everything in my books, and the faith I already had in children's minds was completely reinforced once they were born. They have been a great source of pleasure for me over the years, and it has been wonderful

watching them grow into the intelligent, artistic people that they are. I thank my own parents for the model they provided me with. Just as my dad did with Michael and me, I spent much of their early childhood drawing with them, reading with them and, of course, playing the Shape Game with them!

I believe it is vital that parents spend as much time with their children as they possibly can, and, rather than just observe, actually join in with whatever it is their children enjoy doing. Talking and listening to them is just as important.

Jane and I drew with them all the time, while sharing and commenting on each other's drawings. We tried to encourage this side of their personalities to flourish. It did, and both of them became very good artists. Ellen took fine art to degree level and produced a magnificent final show. The sculptures, photographs and paintings that she produced were brilliant: beautiful, original and skilfully crafted.

Joe also went to art college for a year and showed great promise as a draughtsman, but in the end he decided to study music and English at university. He spent some time in America studying jazz and is now working as a freelance saxophonist, as well as helping me with this memoir! Joe also plays rugby. Just like me, he is a scrum-half, and I have spent many hours watching him play, running the touchline and receiving his passes.

Both my children are very musical, and I have enjoyed watching them play in concerts from a very early age. Contrary to Our Doris's opinion (she was a huge fan of my 'Harry Lime Theme' on guitar),

I can't play a note, but Jane is a professional violinist and has been instrumental in stoking the children's enthusiasm for music. She taught Joe the violin for years (and he became very good), but in the end he fell in love with jazz, which caused him to gravitate towards the saxophone. I too love jazz, and the saxophone in particular, so I am delighted with the path he has taken. Ellen plays the cello and the flute very well, but not as often as she used to. Art has overtaken music for her in the way that music has overtaken art for Joe. Both children have excelled in both of their parents' lines of work, but each has chosen to pursue a different one.

Music remains important to me. It was a particular pleasure when Jane composed music for *Willy the Wimp* and when, in 2010, the composer Luke Bedford set *Willy and Hugh* to music for two packed performances at Wigmore Hall in London.

Jane and I are not together any more, but we are still good friends. Raising children with someone is a very binding experience and it is good that, despite the difficulties of separating, we still appreciate that we have a family together.

Jane now has a partner who is a musician and I have a partner who is an illustrator. It wasn't our different professions that caused the problems between Jane and me, but it is interesting how things have turned out. We are both happy now – far more so knowing that the family is still relatively cohesive. My partner, Hanne Bartholin, is a Danish children's illustrator and author. We enjoy sharing the problems and solutions of producing picture

Above left: illustration, by Joe, 1990
Above right: illustration, by Ellen, 1992
Right: *Frida* by Ellen, 2002

Overleaf: me, c. 1950

books and spending time together with Joe, Ellen and Hanne's daughter, Simone.

I take my work at a leisurely pace these days, and punctuate it with lots of walking, reading and listening to music. I am still a rugby fan, so many Saturday afternoons are spent watching either Joe or Alex (Michael's son) play, or watching the game on the television. Until recently I played cricket on Sunday afternoons for the village that I lived in for twenty years, in a team that has fielded as many as six members of the Browne family at once.

Michael married twice and has five children. He lives happily in a rapidly diminishing household (his three children from his second family are at university). He taught geography at the same girls' grammar school for forty years. He enjoyed his job and was, by all accounts, brilliant at it.

In June 2009 I was delighted to become the Children's Laureate. My aim was to encourage more children to discover and love reading, focusing particularly on the appreciation of picture books, and the reading of both pictures AND words.

I strongly believe that picture books are special. Sometimes I hear parents encouraging their children to read what they call 'proper' books (that's books without pictures), at an earlier and earlier age. This makes me sad, as picture books are perfect for sharing, and not just with the youngest children. As a father, I understand the importance of the bond that develops through reading and talking about picture books with your child. I believe the best picture books leave a tantalising gap between the pictures

and the words, a gap that's filled by the reader's imagination, adding so much to the excitement of the book. Picture books are for everybody at any age, not books to be left behind as we grow older.

One of the things I've tried to encourage is the act of looking. Research has shown that visitors to art galleries spend, on average, thirty seconds looking at each painting, and considerably more time reading the captions. It's an unfortunate element of growing up that we can lose a great deal of contact with our visual imagination, and I hoped to try and change this by encouraging children – and adults – to play the Shape Game.

In the best picture books the pictures contain clues; they tell you what characters are thinking or how they're feeling. By reading these clues we get a far deeper understanding of the story. We have, in

Britain, some of the best picture book makers in the world, and I want to see their books appreciated for what they are – works of art.

In spite of my concerns about the state of picture books, I am optimistic about the future. I realize now more than ever that I am incredibly lucky to love what I do. Straight after finishing art college I was disheartened because it seemed inevitable that in order to make a living from art, I would have to make massive compromises. The experience of doing those advertising jobs made any dreams I once had seem futile. I was getting paid, but the fun of drawing had been taken away. Some of the fun I retrieved when I became a medical illustrator, and I enjoyed making many of the card designs, but it wasn't until I discovered picture books that I learned it was possible to have as much fun with a paint-brush as I had as a child and get paid for it. This is what I love most about my job. What I do now is exactly what I did then: tell stories and draw pictures. Nothing much has changed, not even my approach. Drawing was always my favourite thing to do, and you could say that my career is comparable to other little boys growing up and being paid to play with Lego or dress up as cowboys!

I am also extremely lucky that I have been able to continue 'playing' for a living for so long. I could never stop drawing. Even if I was to give up doing it for a living, I would carry on doing it for pleasure. But doing it for a living is doing it for pleasure, so there really is no reason to stop! It would be fair to say that I have slowed my production rate some-

what, but the ideas are still coming. I am grateful that the job I love is one that I can continue to do until I tire of it.

I still play the Shape Game constantly, perhaps more than ever. My most recent books are classic examples. Silly Billy matures emotionally within the story, and by learning to interpret the world in a more adult way, converting his worries into cares for other people, he plays the Shape Game with his character. *Little Beauty* is the result of me misremembering two stories I had heard and confusing them in my mind. Without realizing it, I played the Shape Game with the two stories in my head and turned them into a book. With *Me and You* I took an existing tale and transformed it by offering another point of view.

The Shape Game is the link throughout my life and work. What started as a trivial pastime, designed to while away wet afternoons, became the nucleus of everything I do. When I am not drawing the shapes on paper, I am drawing them in my head. I play when I am awake and I play when I am asleep. It should drive me mad, but it doesn't. As I get older, my body will of course play a Shape Game with itself, taking its current form and distorting it into that of an old man. Perhaps my mind will change too. Things may become more confusing and I may lose the ability to differentiate between what is real and what is a product of the Shape Game.

But one thing I do know is that I will continue to play for the rest of my life. And that's fine.

Bibliography

Through the Magic Mirror, Hamish Hamilton Children's Books, 1976

A Walk in the Park, Hamish Hamilton Children's Books, 1977

Bear Hunt, Hamish Hamilton Children's Books, 1979

Look What I've Got!, Julia MacRae Books, 1980

Hansel and Gretel, Julia MacRae Books, 1981

Bear Goes to Town, Hamish Hamilton Children's Books, 1982

Gorilla, Julia MacRae Books, 1983

The Visitors Who Came to Stay, written by Annalena McAfee, Hamish Hamilton Children's Books, 1984

Willy the Wimp, Julia MacRae Books, 1984

Knock, Knock, Who's There, written by Sally Grindley, Hamish Hamilton Children's Books, 1985

Willy the Champ, Julia MacRae Books, 1985

Piggybook, Julia MacRae Books, 1986

Kirsty Knows Best, written by Annalena McAfee, Julia MacRae Books, 1987

Alice's Adventures in Wonderland, written by Lewis Carroll, Julia MacRae Books, 1988

Little Bear Book, Hamish Hamilton Children's Books, 1988

I Like Books, Julia MacRae Books, 1988

Things I Like, Julia MacRae Books, 1989

A Bear-y Tale, Hamish Hamilton Children's Books, 1989

The Tunnel, Julia MacRae Books, 1989

Trail of Stones, written by Gwen Strauss, Julia MacRae Books, 1990

Changes, Julia MacRae Books, 1990

Willy and Hugh, Julia MacRae Books, 1991

The Night Shimmy, written by Gwen Strauss, Julia MacRae Books, 1991

Zoo, Julia MacRae Books, 1992

The Big Baby, Julia MacRae Books, 1993

The Topiary Garden, written by Janni Howker, Julia MacRae Books, 1993

The Daydreamer, written by Ian McEwan, Jonathan Cape, 1994

King Kong, from the story conceived by Edgar Wallace and Merian Cooper, Julia MacRae Books, 1994

Willy the Wizard, Julia MacRae Books, 1995

Willy the Dreamer, Walker Books, 1997

Voices in the Park, Doubleday 1998

My Dad, Doubleday, 2000

Willy's Pictures, Walker Books, 2000

The Animal Fair, Walker Books, 2002

The Shape Game, Doubleday, 2003

Into the Forest, Walker Books, 2004

My Mum, Doubleday, 2005

Silly Billy, Walker Books, 2006

My Brother, Doubleday, 2007

Little Beauty, Walker Books, 2008

Me and You, Doubleday, 2010

Play the Shape Game, Walker Books, 2010

Acknowledgements

The author and publishers wish to thank the museums, libraries, archives, publishers and other institutions for their kind permission to reproduce works in their collections and to permit the inclusion of copyright material.

Illustrations from the following books by Anthony Browne are reproduced by kind permission of Walker Books: *Through the Magic Mirror*; *Look What I've Got!*; *Hansel and Gretel*; *Gorilla*; *The Visitors Who Came to Stay*; *Willy the Wimp*; *Willy the Champ*; *Piggybook*; *Alice's Adventures in Wonderland*; *The Tunnel*; *Changes*; *Willy the Dreamer*; *Willy's Pictures*; *Silly Billy*; *Little Beauty*

Illustrations from *King Kong* on pages 4, 17, 38-9, 76-7, 92-5 copyright © 1994 Julia MacRae Books

Family photographs, pp13, 16, 19, 30-31, 100-1, 232 and 237, reproduced by permission of the author

'The Mad Hatter's Tea Party' from *The Adventures of Alice in Wonderland* by Lewis Carroll and illustrated by Sir John Tenniel, p22; image from www.fromoldbooks.org used by permission

Newspaper extracts, pp27 and 36, from the Halifax Evening Courier, reproduced by permission

Le Model Rouge (The Red Model) (oil on canvas) by Magritte, René (1898-1967), p29; Ex-Edward James Foundation, Sussex, UK / The Bridgeman Art Library. Copyright © ADAGP, Paris and DACS, London 2011

Lying Figure with Hypodermic Syringe, 1963 (oil on canvas) by Bacon, Francis (1909-92), p40; University Art Museum, Berkeley, USA / Peter Willi / The Bridgeman Art Library. Copyright © The Estate of Francis Bacon. All rights reserved, DACS 2011

Medical illustrations, pp49 and 51, copyright © The Department of Clinical Photography & Medical Illustration, Central Manchester University Hospitals NHS Foundation Trust. Reproduced by permission of The University of Manchester, United Kingdom and CMFT NHS Trust

Gordon Fraser greetings cards, pp46-47, 53, 54-55, reproduced by kind permission of Hallmark Cards plc

Illustrations from *Bear Hunt*, pp67 and 68, copyright © 1979 Anthony Browne; reproduced by permission of Puffin Books

'Under the Rug' from *The Mysteries of Harris Burdick* by Chris Van Allsburg copyright © 1984 by Chris Van Allsburg, p140. Reprinted by permission of Houghton Mifflin Harcourt Publishing Company. All rights reserved.

Mona Lisa, c.1503-6 (oil on panel) by Vinci, Leonardo da (1452-1519), p152; Louvre, Paris, France / Giraudon / The Bridgeman Art Library

The Birth of Venus, c.1485 (tempera on canvas) by Botticelli, Sandro (1444/5-1510), p153; Galleria degli Uffizi, Florence, Italy / Giraudon / The Bridgeman Art Library

Studio photograph, p162, and photograph of Joe and Ellen, p231, copyright © 2010 Anthony Browne

Past and Present, No.1, 1858 by Augustus Egg, p175, copyright © 2010 Tate, London

'The Meeting' or 'Have a Nice Day, Mr Hockney', 1981-3 by Peter Blake, p180, copyright © Peter Blake. All rights reserved, DACS 2011. Photograph copyright © 2011 Tate, London

Photographs of 'El Mundo de Anthony Browne' exhibition, pp197-201, copyright © 1996 Anthony Browne

Photograph of Anthony Browne and Tayo Shima, p201, copyright © 2001 IBBY

Photographs, pp203 and 235, copyright © 2010 Katie Vandyck

Illustrations on p234 by Ellen Browne and Joe Browne reproduced by permission of the artists

Every effort has been made to trace the holders of copyright material in this book. If any query should arise it should be addressed to the publishers.

Previous page: *My Brother*, Doubleday, 2007
Right: *The Shape Game*, Doubleday, 2003

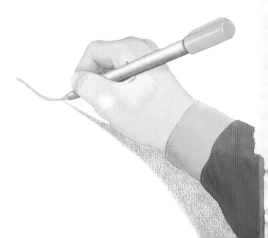